SACRED
KNOTS

SACRED KNOTS

Create, adorn, and transform
through the art of knotting

LISE SILVA GOMES

Photographs by Erin Conger

ROOST BOOKS

Roost Books
An imprint of Shambhala Publications, Inc.
4720 Walnut Street
Boulder, Colorado 80301
roostbooks.com

Cover art: Lise Silva Gomes
Cover design: Kara Plikaitis
Interior design: Nami Kurita

9 8 7 6 5 4 3 2 1

First Edition
Printed in China

✢This edition is printed on acid-free paper that meets the American National Standards Institute Z39.48 Standard.
♻Shambhala Publications makes every effort to print on recycled paper. For more information please visit www.shambhala.com.
Roost Books is distributed worldwide by Penguin Random House, Inc., and its subsidiaries.

Library of Congress Cataloging-in-Publication Data
Names: Gomes, Lise Silva, author. | Conger, Erin, photographer.
Title: Sacred knots: create, adorn, and transform through the art of knotting /
Lise Silva Gomes; photographs by Erin Conger.
Description: First edition. | Boulder, Colorado: Roost Books, 2020.
Identifiers: LCCN 2019046878 | ISBN 9781611807776 (trade paperback)
Subjects: LCSH: Knots and splices. | Ropework.
Classification: LCC TT840.R66 G66 2020 | DDC 746.42/2—dc23
LC record available at https://lccn.loc.gov/2019046878

FOR
FAMILY, FRIENDS & PHYLLIS FISHER
WITH GRATITUDE FOR THE MANY
STUDENTS WHO TAUGHT ME TO TEACH
AND THE ANCESTORS WHO CULTIVATED
THE PRACTICE

CONTENTS

Preface: My Personal Journey in Knotting ix

Introduction: Knotting a Thread from Past to Present xiii

PART ONE
KNOTTING BASICS
1

The Materials   3

A Guide to Knotting   28

Basic Knots   39

    Square Knot   42

    Double Coin   44

    Cross Knot   46

    Sun Cycle   48

    Sailor's Breastplate   50

    Cloud Knot   52

    Weaver's Plait   54

    Plafond   56

    Pipa Knot   58

Finishing and
Embellishing Techniques   60

PART TWO
KNOTTING PROJECTS
75

Pipa Knot Earrings   77

Mãe d'Água Necklace
and Earrings Set   79

Knot Sequence:
Manifesting Dreams   83

Satin Bookmark   88

Sun Worshipper
Statement Necklace   92

Cross Knot
Stacking Bracelet   99

Colorblock Woven
Knot Panel   103

Double Coin Curtain   110

Knot Appliqué Jacket   117

PART THREE
KNOTTING AS A PERSONAL PRACTICE
125

Knotting as a Meditation   126

Practicing Intention   129

Making Affirmations   131

Fiber Practice Journal:
Intention Log   132

Knotting for Relaxation   135

Practicing Creativity   140

Recording your
Personal Journey   142

Resources   148

Acknowledgments   151

About the Author   152

PREFACE

My Personal Journey in Knotting

As I look around my studio, a rainbow of dyed rope hangs from the walls, soft sculptural knots cover worktables like super-sized primordial organisms, and a tangle of cord spreads like a web across the floor. It's the kind of mess of color and chaos that feels alive with possibility. The many years of maintaining a personal creative practice with knots unleashed a well of creative joy. My journey through knotting has been more like a serendipitous fall through the rabbit hole than a plotted and mapped quest; in allowing myself to freely explore tiny signposts that caused my heart to leap, I was able to find my own creative path. I immersed myself in the long history of fiber art and knotting, and once I learned the foundational principles, I started on the path of playful experimentation, making big personal breakthroughs, designing my own knots, combining elements from different fiber mediums, and developing my own jewelry and wall-hanging aesthetic. Even as I began to immerse myself in the quirky world of knotting, I had no idea how much power this personal practice would have to shape my life: supplementing my meditation study, connecting me to a much-needed ancestral practice at a time when screens began to dominate modern life, and providing me with a therapeutic creative outlet to explore ideas.

My knot journey began in 2012 when I started to collect quirky 1970s- and 1980s-era macramé pamphlets from thrift stores. Although they didn't seem to serve any purpose other than delighting and amusing me, I didn't hesitate to start collecting these little booklets. When I finally started to test my hand at making the projects, I preferred to go off script and experiment. Always feeling the pull to improvise from the standard directions, I found that most of these endeavors didn't amount to beautiful final pieces; instead, this process served as an important way for me to absorb some essential skills and engage in trial and error to make new discoveries and realize my own aesthetic preferences. Learning this new creative skill on my own, outside of traditional classes or the gaze of social media, was also incredibly important to my creative development.

Those macramé booklets became my gateway to the world of knotting. Eventually, I found the simple repetition of the basic macramé knots to be engaging for my busy hands but not engaging enough for my restless mind. I also found that sometimes the magnitude of the tiny knots required could be tiresome on my hands and that the cord lengths necessary to make most pieces could be impossible to obtain or incredibly expensive in the vintage deadstock cords I was using. I began to wonder . . . what if instead of making hundreds or thousands of tiny, simple knots, I just made one big, intricate knot? As I dug deeper, I learned about Celtic knots, sailor's knots, Chinese knotting, Korean knotting, and the knotting traditions that stem from just about every culture in the world.

After a year or so of practicing privately, I began to wear my necklace creations, share the results of what I was making, and talk about the legacy of the traditional knots behind the pieces. For the first couple years, I mainly translated traditional knots into wall hangings and jewelry, but soon after, I found designing my own knots to be more fulfilling. To my surprise, people actually wanted to purchase my designs, and as my business grew, I began to teach knotting techniques and incorporate meditation principles that I relied on for my own creative practice. Teaching a craft has been one of my greatest learning experiences; it has been humbling and empowering and has unveiled the creative process to me in a new way. Many of my insights through teaching were in seeing myself mirrored in others—by taking distance from ourselves we can get perspective. The insights I was receiving from teaching were also a reflection of insights received from meditation. Meditation offers a perspective that ripples through every layer of life and has a close relationship with creativity, so incorporating it into both my knot practice and my method of teaching felt natural.

Knotting, for me, is more than the end result. It is my creative practice, a puzzle that invigorates my mind, a connection to ancestral legacy, and a mode

of meditation that inhabits the space between work and play. The universe of knotting techniques contains so much technical variation and so many styles of practice that it can be challenging or relaxing, elevating or grounding, mindful or mindless—all depending on what I need in the moment and which kind of technique I choose. Knots can range from the functional to the wearable to the symbolic to the purely decorative, but the constant throughout each project is the opportunity to tap further into myself. Knotting is a framework that allows us space to play, to challenge ourselves, to ground ourselves, and to learn. No matter from which area of the world your ancestry stems, there is a knotting practice unique to your background to explore.

My dream is for this book to not only teach you the fundamentals of knotting, but also initiate the start of a meditative, grounding creative practice for you. I share basic tools and techniques to get you fluent in the vocabulary of knotting, provide some information on the legacy of knotting to center your practice, suggest ways to innovate and experiment with the medium, and hold space for the mystery of knots to ignite your imagination. Rather than serving as an encyclopedic overview of knotting or a technical manual for a particular tradition, this book shares an overview of the diverse possibilities of knotting and guides you to discover your own creative knotting practice; you may choose to use it as a companion to other resources where you can explore specific traditional knot techniques that pique your interest.

As you embark on the exercises in this book, take special note of the preoccupations, questions, personal themes, or life events you bring with you. As you are opening this new door to knotting, what is on your mind and where are you on your journey? Is there anything you want to manifest or express? Is there something you want to hang in your home or studio or around your neck that serves as a reminder for a personal theme, goal, or milestone? Take a moment to listen as your inner voice softly answers each of these questions. And as you begin, detach a bit from the idea of an end product and connect deeper to your breath and the direction in which your inner compass pulls you.

INTRODUCTION

Knotting a Thread from Past to Present

The practice of knotting offers us powerful metaphors for our lives. Through knotting we are able to play out the greatest cosmic principles of connection, balance, transformation, and release with a simple strand of cord, and we are rewarded with ornate designs that parallel sacred geometry. Tension and opposition allow the knot to take shape, while the unity of the cord is the hidden principle behind the design.

THE HISTORY OF KNOTS

From the spiritual to the functional to the decorative, knots have served roles as diverse as a tool for gathering food to a storytelling medium. Knots have held a central role in many of the world's civilizations in ceremony and ritual; there were magic knots for casting spells in Rome, knots for marriage in Russia, knots for wish manifestation in China, ceremonies surrounding untying knots during birthing practices in India and West Africa, knotted spiritual protection amulets in Egypt, and knots for recording village and family history throughout indigenous cultures of South America. The widespread utility of knots stems from their accessibility both as a way to convey meaning through visual symbols and by the humble and abundant nature of the materials used to make them. Knots have been tied in just about every strand of material—from plant fibers like vines and seagrass to hair and fur—since humanity's earliest beginnings. And because knots can convey meanings that don't require literacy to decipher, knotting was a simple way for humanity at all literacy levels, incomes, and environments to convey information.

Several cultures developed extensive knotting vocabularies, but little has been well-preserved over time. Industrialization had a disastrous effect on slow crafts like knotting. In addition, the ravages of colonialism in the Americas,

Southeast Asia, and Africa contributed to the tragic loss of legacies and artifacts for so many of our ancestral traditions, including the practice of knotting. By the 1970s, dedicated artisans and art historians around the world, like Lydia Chen, took up the mantel to recover knot traditions by speaking with elders and studying artifacts. Today, the most popular knotting traditions that remain are Chinese knotting, Celtic knotting, sailor's knots, and macramé (North Africa).

With physical records dating back to 500 B.C.E., knotting is well documented in Chinese culture, hanging from clothing, framing designs, and tying back hair in reliefs and sculptures. The brilliance in concept and technical mastery ranges from re-creations of wildlife (Dragonfly and Butterfly Knots) to concepts of luck and success (the Good Luck Knot) and is truly awe-inspiring. This enduring knot tradition, typically created with silky, fine cords, has graced community celebrations and bestows luck for new beginnings, spiritual affirmations, and wish manifestation. Small, intricate red knots can be spotted widely during the Chinese New Year celebrations every February in communities around the world.

Celtic knotting carries a sense of heritage and spirituality through polytheistic belief, the natural world, lore, and family lineage. Celtic knots are widely re-created in metal jewelry today because, unlike other forms of knotting, the original designs were engraved into metal and stone or etched into other flat surfaces like wood or paper rather than created with cord. Celtic knots commonly appear like sinuous vines or branches and are often intricate like a labyrinth. Because they were usually drawn in two dimensions and not held to the limits of an actual cord, most Celtic knot designs do not easily translate to physical cord unless one cuts multiple strands and glues or sews the loops in place to replicate the flat, intricate design where sections of the linework appear and disappear in and out of the design without a discernible pathway. Nevertheless, Celtic knotwork has a very distinct aesthetic defined by plaits, spirals, key patterns, zoomorphics, and plant sinews. Ancient Celtic designs were appropriated by Christian artisans around 450 B.C.E. and many of the pagan meanings were lost.

Possibly the most well-documented historical knot tradition is a global hybrid called sailor's knots, which is the collective effort of sailors traveling, learning, and sharing information. Designing nautical vessels and problem-solving at sea resulted in a large vocabulary of utilitarian knots that are still in wide use both functionally and decoratively. Sailor's knots range from compact, load-bearing knots to beautiful, decorative designs called "fancy knotwork," a creative endeavor to pass the long hours on the boat. The clever knotwork designs

KNOTS, SPLICES
AND FANCY WORK

By C. L. SPENCER

the sailors created were used for decorating ships, sharing lore, or symbolically pining for friends and family they left behind. While functional knots used daily aboard the ship were more compact and not as showy, they also held a sacred place for the workers who used them while at sea, because correctly tying knots from memory could be a matter of life and death. The *Ashley Book of Knots*, first published in 1944 to finally document centuries of sailor's knots on the page, contains eleven years of knot research and is one of the world's most extensive knot records, cataloging nearly four thousand designs and still available in print today.

Lastly, macramé, one of the most popular knotting styles in the modern-day United States, originates in the Middle East and North Africa, where the creation of beautiful knotted fringe surfaces helped to protect from dust and buffer the wind. When North African cultures dominated areas of Europe from the eighth to tenth centuries, their aesthetic influences were assimilated throughout the continent. Macramé, traditionally done in twine, jute, hemp, leather, or yarn, has remained one of the most enduring forms of knotting because of its easy technique and endless potential for two-dimensional artwork like curtains and decorative textiles or three-dimensional objects like lamp shades, dresses, and market bags. Macramé is created by tying simple knots (commonly variations of the square knot) across rope strands in alternating row patterns, working down strands of hanging rope from left to right and right to left until each row is filled. Macramé saw a resurgence during the Victorian era and again in the 1960s and 1970s. Currently in its third resurgence, it is one of the most popular do-it-yourself fiber trends shared online and at craft fairs around the globe.

Aside from these popular forms of knotting, there are fascinating, lesser-known traditions to explore from other regions of the world. An important indigenous knotting legacy of South America is the *quipu*, or "talking knots," a system of knotted strings that could serve as a calendar or as a database for information such as the demographics of the village over time, accounting, and inventory. Similar ancient knotted recording systems were created in other locations, such as China and Polynesia, but the word "quipu" and its aesthetic relate to indigenous South Americans, primarily the Caral-Supe, the Wari, and the Incan communities of the Andes. Constructed either hanging vertically or spread flat and circular on a surface like a mop, a quipu was created by placing knots at different places on a colorful dyed cotton string or spun wool to represent numerical data increments. Each string may have represented an increment of time; its color, another piece of information; and each knot and its placement, an event and quantity. A quipu was read similar to a graph with an x-axis and a y-axis at each knot across the strings, but only by its keeper, an elder village historian who held its key. Incorporating possibly hundreds or thousands of strings, quipus demonstrated advanced mathematical systems and information storage. Spanish colonial forces destroyed thousands of quipus, but several natural history museums across the Americas have preserved intact quipus.

Another knot-based mnemonic device is the *sona* sand paintings of central Africa, specifically of the Chokwe and Luchazi people of Angola, Zambia, and the Congo. Sona patterns (*lusona* in the singular) are the intersection of mathematics, art, education, and storytelling. Similar to Celtic knots, they were often designed on two-dimensional surfaces, drawn in sand as temporary works of art, problem-solving, or storytelling, rather than made with actual cording. The infinite linework of sona usually does not have a beginning or end and was also used by women designing basketry. The knots are made by drawing curving lines around a matrix of dots, using the principle of mirrors to create symmetry. Often representing animals, sona patterns look similar to constellations, using familiar symbols drawn around points as a mnemonic device. Intrinsic in the knotwork are principles of geometry and Eulerian cycles, as sona patterns predate knot theory developed by European mathematicians.

Moving northeast, there are a variety of other knotting traditions, including *maedup* knotting of Korea, Japanese Mizuhiki knotting, and sinnets and netting in Polynesian cultures. Maedup is similar to Chinese knotting but uses different diagramming models, and the technique is entirely done in hand, without the use of any tools (Chinese knotting encourages the use of pins, knotting board, and crochet hooks). Korean knotting has seen a resurgence in the last few decades and can be seen today as a decorative element on accessories. The Japanese knotting tradition of Mizuhiki is also closely related to Chinese and Korean knotting but is distinctly different in material, process, and origin. Traditionally made with rice paper cording that is stiffened with starch and painted, Mizuhiki is often used as a decorative element, such as a gift topper or small sculptural keepsake to celebrate an event like a wedding. The origin has been traced to the beautiful knots *samurai* used to tie back their hair.

Cousins to the knotting family are nets, sinnets, and braids, which are present in cultures around the world but have a particularly rich legacy in Polynesia. These facets of knotting, closely overlapping in technique to basketry and macramé, involve plaiting natural plant fibers like seagrass and palm leaves. From fishing nets to clothing, architecture, fans, and home décor, the remnants of ancient knotting and plaiting have been integrated into the modern culture on the islands.

The global variations in knotting reveal the vast possibilities of the medium and offer us a rich historical and cultural education. Knot practices reflect the way of life of the cultures that developed them and demonstrate how brilliant, resourceful, creative, committed, community oriented, and hopeful our ancestors were; the remains of lost traditions that were suppressed, destroyed, and overlooked give us an eye-opening education on the violence and inequality that have been inflicted upon indigenous cultures throughout history. For these reasons, we should engage with traditional knotting practices with a deep respect for the cultures that created them and gratitude for the great effort of the elders to preserve them against the sway of modernization, commercialism, and colonialism. The knot traditions that remain result from a web of ancestral storytelling, resistance, and documentation to keep the skill sets in our collective consciousness. Traditional knotting techniques are avenues you may want to research to connect to your ancestral lineage or to reflect on to ground you in your personal practice. It is important to note that when traditions stem from historically oppressed cultures, it may not be appropriate for outsiders of the culture to practice the craft, in which case you can respectfully engage with it from a purely educational perspective and as a supporter of artisans of that community who continue the tradition. If you choose to practice a traditional technique, it should be studied from an elder who represents the community from which the tradition stems.

KNOTTING AS A PERSONAL PRACTICE

We always have intentions when we begin a new creative project, but we rarely take the time to articulate what they are. When we are too focused on the results and not deeply connected to our creative journey, we can spiral into feeling inadequate, engaging in negative self-talk, blaming, or abandoning creative projects altogether as a failure. The truth is not that we are incapable or doomed to fail, but rather that we didn't take time to acknowledge what was drawing us to the pursuit and why we were pursuing it. Our intention can serve as a compass guiding us toward the most effective path in our creative practice.

Setting intention is an essential part of transforming just about anything you do from an *activity* to a *practice* (more on this in part 3). "Practice" is a term I use a lot in this book to describe an orientation toward crafting where the time you spend with your materials is driven by a desire for personal growth and

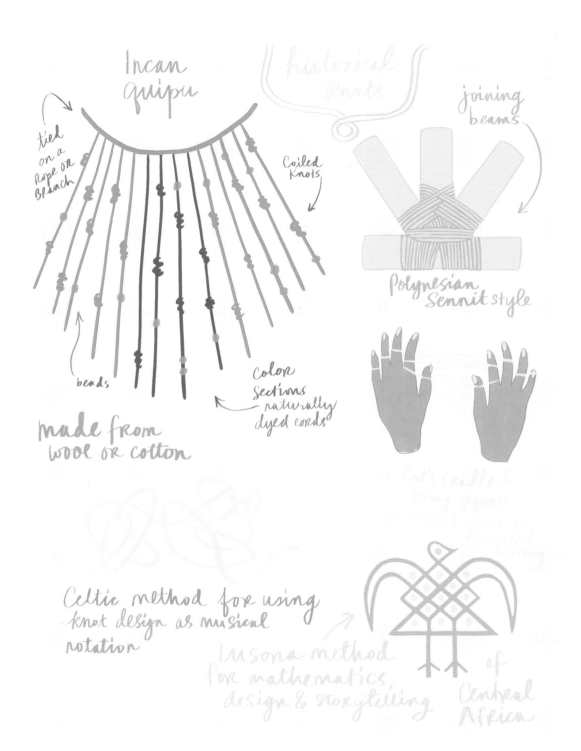

Incan quipu

historical knots

joining beams

tied on a Rope or Branch

Coiled Knots

Polynesian Sennit style

beads

color Sections naturally dyed cords

made from wool or cotton

Celtic method for using knot design as musical notation

Lusona method for mathematics, design & storytelling

of Central Africa

connection to one's inner self rather than an external achievement or end result. When we are crafting, we are often working on it from the outside in—meaning, we are thinking aesthetically about how it will appear to others and focused on referencing others' styles while creating or designing with an attempt to appeal to an imaginary audience's perspective. Carving out some creative time that is strictly a personal practice allows us to enter into an activity concerned with the means, not the end, the journey rather than the product. We can still maintain our creative endeavors that are product focused and audience focused while also setting aside some personal free play to connect with our inner self and generate fresh, deeply inspired ideas. Entering a creative mode that is just for us to experience in the moment, not conceptualized as an amazing photo to post online nor aligned with a certain style, will unlock a new channel for inspiration to flow.

You can set intention in the beginning of your practice through many ways: doing a few minutes of breathwork or meditation, saying a prayer of intention, pulling some oracle cards to set the tone, or writing down some goals or affirmations for the session. For those drawn to crafts with historical components, like knotting, gratitude and ancestral connection are powerful forms of intention. Simply sitting down as you are—knotting with the intention of imagining or connecting to the lives of ancestors hundreds or thousands of years ago, making the very same knot as you are sitting here, thankful for the wisdom which you can access today—can be a very grounding practice. You can find so many symbols and meaningful stories behind the creation of historical knots, and each knot listed in this book has a brief description of its origin and meaning.

USING THIS BOOK

Your reservoir for creative potential is infinite, extending far deeper than you could even imagine. In fact, part of the elation of the creative process is surprising yourself with what creations flow out of you. You are capable of creating fresh, new innovations, expressing deep wisdom and insight, and capturing a mood or perception with an accuracy beyond your conscious understanding. These things are all waiting to be unlocked, but the doors that bar them are largely mental barriers and distractions that prevent you from reaching deep enough into your pocket to find the keys. Creativity references your experiences, ideas, and influences, which are the result of interactions or observations of other people; however, when you sit down to create your own work, you will be engaging in a process that has no direction or even conceivable end point.

While step-by-step tutorials are important starting points for skill building, I encourage you to step beyond the instructions in this book to make your own design choices. When you engage in a creative project without a guide, there can be an underlying tension and questioning: Where am I going? Am I wasting expensive materials? How long will it take? When is this going to be done? Will this all fit neatly? Will this look good? But pushing through the unknown, learning to steer yourself away from the destructive mental self-talk, tapping into your deepest sense of self, and committing to your own decisions can bring you some of the most magical results. It's also a life-changing method of personal development that forces you to address questions like: What do I like? What is my perspective? What do I want to explore deeper?

As you work through the knots in this book, both the basic knots and the larger projects, allow yourself to stray at times or take a meandering path to experiment along the way. I encourage you to record notes on your experiments—mistakes and happy accidents alike—in a fiber journal that you create. Sometimes the meandering mistakes, both good and bad, provide helpful tips on which directions to head or not to head as you continue to experiment.

"Every adversity, every failure, every heartache carries with it the seed of an equal or greater benefit," said Napoleon Hill. Creative pursuits aren't always easy, and they are often a long and winding road; however, the commitment to a creative practice is one of the most enriching and satisfying ones you could make. Stay focused on the means rather than the end, the process rather than the product as you work. Think about shaping a practice space for yourself and keeping that time sacred. As most of us are surrounded by screens that act like windows on the world for peek out at others' lives, a creative space that banishes devices may be the only time in the day where we aren't looking outside of ourselves for communication, validation, answers, or inspiration. Relish the opportunity to dive deep within and see what manifests.

I also have a caveat about the Internet in regard to your creative process: Don't let it obscure, replace, or stunt your own creativity. We are often tempted to turn to Internet tutorials for every twist and turn of the creative process and when we get stuck creatively, however, when we sit with our frustration for a bit, our creativity can push us into a new stratosphere of ideas and techniques. Also, when you pull yourself out of the creative zone to look up something online, you are not only breaking your meditative mind state, but you are also turning away from your inward focus to look outside yourself for ideas. While the Internet can be a great aid to you, especially during the educational phase while you are learning about knotting, I encourage you to try to avoid using it during your creative process when you are freely experimenting. I also suggest sitting with the frustrating parts of your projects to see if flexing your creative muscles in that space presents you with new discoveries or confidence in your ability to resolve obstacles in your own way.

Learn the fundamentals to gain a vocabulary and then use these building blocks to speak your own truth. Discovering your own method to accomplish your ideas is an easy, natural way to develop your style. Nothing feels better than manifesting your own unique magic. Don't feel you have to reinvent the wheel, but at the same time, don't let this age of abundant do-it-yourself tutorials rob you of your creativity either. Copying can be fun and educational, but it is fundamentally soulless. Always pay love and respect to the fruits of your imagination and other's imaginations by being aware of the difference between imitation and inspiration. This guide is about learning from thousands of years of shared collective consciousness and using diagrams and tutorials to get you up and running while nurturing space to express your own unique dreams and spirit once you have the mechanics down pat.

PART ONE

KNOTTING BASICS

There is something so satisfying about working with cording. The tactile experience of manipulating physical materials feels like a respite when much of our day takes place on a screen. Begin your knotting practice by choosing your cording, gathering tools and extra materials to embellish your piece, learning how to read diagrams, understanding the basic principles of knotting, and setting up your workspace.

THE MATERIALS

Materials are often a defining characteristic of an artist's signature aesthetic, and finding the right materials can be a journey as personal as the subject matter itself. Discovering your voice in the medium through material choice is a hugely satisfying part of the process of creation and holds space for the vision to begin. As you design, the ways in which the subtle characteristics of your material respond to the techniques you use will have an invisible hand in your work. Many of my designs stem from just letting the materials tell me what they want to do, which I know sounds very abstract. "Listening to the materials" means closely observing how they respond to manipulation, how they hold shapes, how they feel in your hands, and what pathways they take easily. Materials can be the difference between your piece looking overworked or effortless. If you overwork a material, it usually means you are forcing it to do a technique for which it is not suited. Pick out cording that catches your eye and challenge yourself to see what techniques or knot styles it does best. By playfully experimenting, you will organically develop your own unique aesthetic and may find yourself forming strong opinions on the way certain elements look together. Hands-on creative play with a wide range of materials will enhance your creative growth and up the sophistication of your designs. Your imagination is your only limit.

Cording

Cording is the only absolutely essential material for knotting, and your selection of cording is probably the most important factor of how your knotted creations will look. You'll want to experiment with different cord samples to see how they respond to the types of designs you are interested in creating. Choose a favorite knot that is most emblematic of your taste: it may be the Weaver's Plait, which is very flat, ornate, and woven; or it may be a chain of chunky Cross Knots. Test different cords by making the same knot in each cord type; then, evaluate your knot samples, noticing that they may appear wildly different in each material, texture, and diameter—sometimes even unrecognizable as the same design.

Every type of cording has certain strengths and weaknesses and was often created for very specific effects or tasks. Understanding how cords respond to different techniques, how you can exploit their weaknesses into a new exciting style, or how you can accent their strengths is all part of the experimentation process. For example, twist cords often have a tendency to quite literally twist when knotted tightly, which can be very annoying if you are looking for a flat knot design. On the other hand, if you use the twist factor for the benefit of your piece, you might create a long chain of square knots in your piece, noticing that if you keep going with more length, the annoying twist turns into an amazing spiral. You now have discovered this swirling DNA tendril effect that will leave people wondering how in the world you made the rope spiral like that, when in fact, it was an "error" you turned into a design element. Trying the same knotted designs in different cording is a great way to get a lot of design mileage, technical challenge, and new creative ideas from a small knot vocabulary.

TYPES OF CORDING

A veritable feast of delicious cord is available today: shiny, soft, matte, round, flat, braided, twisted, silky, raw, fuzzy, smooth, hollow, stuffed. . . . Every type of cord brings something different to your projects. The varieties of cording I recommend for beginners are ¼-inch cotton braid rope, 550 paracord, and 2 mm to 4 mm satin rattail.

Cotton braid at any diameter has a great feel in your hands while you are knotting; it is soft yet rigid enough to maintain shape, and it is commonly available in cream and black, which makes it versatile for a variety of color palettes. At ¼-inch diameter, cotton braid is a thick cord that isn't expensive or overwhelming to handle.

Paracord is a durable and knot-friendly nylon cord developed for use by parachuters and military personnel, and it is widely available in a variety of bright colors for children's jewelry projects.

Satin rattail, available in synthetic or natural fiber, is the cord of choice for Chinese knotting and makes elegant knot jewelry. While rattail is more pliable than the other cords, meaning it doesn't hold shape as well, it has a more polished and high-end look than industrial cords like most rope and paracord.

Although these cords are classic knotting materials, widely available in craft stores and hardware stores, they may or may not be the cords you envision using to make your dream projects. For beginners, I recommend starting out with them to learn the basics, test out ideas, and draft projects before using more expensive or more challenging cords.

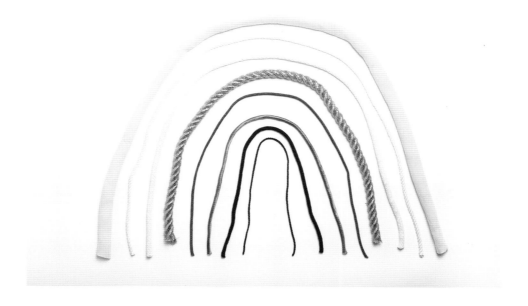

Beyond the basics, this list demonstrates the variety of cords you may want to explore:

Hemp	Jute	Sailing rope
Soutache	Twine/string	Paracord
Seagrass	Cotton braid	Vintage macramé cord
Round leather cord	Waxed cotton/linen	Sash cord
Suede ribbon	Silk cord	Weeping cord
Sisal rope	Upholstery cord	Stuffed fabric tubes
Bungee cord	Basquetry cord	Yarn
Piping	Micro-macramé cord	Polypropylene
Cotton twist rope	Gimp	

CORD CONSIDERATIONS

Consider these four main aspects of cording when making your selection: texture, type of fiber, cost, and scale. Let's take a look at each.

Texture

To a large degree, the texture of your cord will be determined by the material from which it's made; however, you may find quite a few variations within the same material. Cords made from cotton or wool may have a "halo," a soft fuzziness around the circumference, or a "tooth," a slight grip to the surface. Silky cords like satin, silk, cotton, or rayon can vary from roughly textured surfaces with tooth to smooth surfaces as cool and slippery as a wet noodle.

You may also be drawn to a particular cord due to its rigidity and the resulting effects on the aesthetics of your creations. For example, a very soft, pliable cord like yarn will create gentle, floppy shapes, whereas compact, rigid jute rope will create taut shapes and support lots of negative space in a design. Working with these more or less rigid cords will change the feel and process as well. Yarn is easy on the hands but can be difficult for tying ornate knots due to its softness and lack of shape, whereas jute can burn the hands but is very easy to

left to Right:

felted alpaca
braided cotton
3mm cotton
     macramé cord
Cotton piping
dyed twine
waxed cotton
     cord
Cotton twist
     macramé
     rope
Single strand
     macramé
     rope
Rope hand-
     wrapped with
     ribbon yarn
Raffia

knot because its rigidity makes it easy to manipulate. If you decide to work with a coarse material, opt for protection for your hands. Macramé artists who work with jute wear gloves or wrap their hands in bandages before knotting.

Textures also vary depending on how the cords were manufactured. People frequently ask me what kind of rope I use because my cord of choice, a smooth braid rope, is not as common as twist rope, which is a popular nautical style with a bumpy texture often used in macramé. Twist rope, also called "laid rope," is made by twisting two fibers together, much like yarn. It tends to be compact and rigid, which could work to your advantage or against it depending on your project. Due to the spiraling twist running down its length, the texture may complement or detract from your design. People who attempt to wrap twist rope in yarn or fabric strips may love or hate the twist texture that is accentuated. If you want the texture of your rope to be less conspicuous in your design, you may want to go with a smooth-textured cord like a braided rope. Braided rope has an intricate braided weave and is often hollow like a tube, which allows it to gently depress when squeezed. Another choice, a solid braid, is generally stuffed to maintain its full roundness. Whether your cord is hollow or solid will determine how chunky or flat your knots appear.

Fiber: Natural and Synthetic

The most basic aspect of cord is the raw material from which it is made. Natural fibers can be plant based or animal based and have a spectacular range of textures. Plant-based fibers include cotton, hemp, jute, seagrass, and even tencel and rayon, which are made from wood pulp and often incorrectly categorized as synthetic. Animal-based fibers consist largely of particular proteins and include silk, wool, and yarns such as cashmere. Natural fibers offer the gamut from coarse, matte textures to romantic, satiny sheens, depending on the fiber and processing. Natural fiber farming and processing methods are art forms that have been honed for thousands of years, so high-quality natural fibers are expensive.

By contrast, synthetic fibers like polyester, acrylic, nylon, and spandex are made from plastic through scientific processes. These fibers are inexpensive and usually have a high shine, stretch, and some degree of impenetrability.

Beyond the sensory experience of the type of fiber you use is the understanding of textile production and how taxing it is on the planet. Both mass-produced natural and synthetic fibers go through wasteful, inefficient production processes, but the amount of nonbiodegradable waste and plastic microfiber shedding that synthetic fabrics contribute to the ecosystem is undeniably devastating. Picture all the tiny fiber particles we can breathe when lifting a freshly laundered blanket over the bed, sending hundreds of little fuzzies into the air; if the blanket is polyester, these fibers are essentially tiny ribbons of plastic. The process of producing, wearing, breathing in, laundering, and dumping synthetic fibers leaves traces in our water, our food, and our bodies. Just as I try to minimize buying new synthetic clothes and household items, I similarly try to minimize the place they have within my own fiber creations to avoid contributing too greatly to the production of plastic through my material purchases. As artists, we also hope the pieces we make won't someday end up in the junkyard, but over the decades things like that do happen to vintage wall art and jewelry for various reasons, and contributing more immortal plastic to the earth isn't a great idea. That brings us to the other side of the coin: longevity.

Natural fibers do not last long without special care. Moths, sunlight, wind, and temperature can all slowly degrade natural fibers, and that is part of the beauty of the art form. Keeping your natural fiber creations away from direct sunlight, wind, insect infestations, and so on will definitely help to keep your pieces intact over time. The longevity and robustness of your piece may certainly be a concern—particularly if you are making an outdoor decoration or piece for a public space that will have to withstand heavy traffic—and natural fibers won't be the best choice for those projects. Many artists who work with synthetic materials do so by salvaging clearance, thrift, vintage, and "junk" materials and, in doing so, create pieces with a strong inherent message about sustainability and the alchemy of transforming trash into treasure.

Scale: Thickness and Length

While finding your materials, keep in mind the scale of the cord, measured by its diameter. Fine linen cords used for micro-macramé can be just 1 millimeter thick, whereas an industrial rope used for sailing knots can be up to 2 inches thick. Jewelry cords tend to be finer, more expensive, and produce softer knots, which require more sewing or tight, detailed knots to retain their shape. Utility cords tend to give a crafty, rustic, or industrial feel as they produce stiffer, larger knots in rugged beiges, natural cotton neutrals, or neon futuristic synthetics. Again, the plumpness of the cord will also be determined by whether it is hollow or solid. When you knot, the intersections of cord will either flatten upon one another with the tension if the cord is hollow or remain rigid and appear plump if the cord is solid. This also means that as you knot with a hollow cord the dimension will slightly shrink with the tension, resulting in a smaller finished knot than one

1/4" cotton
braid Rope

1/4" cotton
twist Rope

5mm cotton
drawstring

1/2" metallic
twist Rope

2mm silk
twist cord

1" stuffed
fabric cord

2mm Satin
Rattail

6mm Stuffed
silk cord

6mm paracord

tied with a solid cord. Whichever cord you choose will come down to aesthetic preference: how chunky or flat you want your design to look and how the cord holds the knot shapes.

The length of your final piece will be a factor in the scale. For example, if you choose a 1-inch-diameter rope and create a chain of knots that result in a 5-foot-long piece, the cord won't appear as chunky as a 12-inch-long piece using that same 1-inch-diameter rope. In general, a larger-diameter cord is generally more expensive, so cord diameter, length, and budget will all go hand in hand. One way to add bulk to your piece when you are using a thin cord is to stack multiple strands on top of one another.

The easiest way to cut your cord for multiple strands is to do so in halves, or multiples of two. Take the entire length of cord and fold it in half. If you were to make a cut at the center of your halved cord, you would have two even strands. To do so neatly, wrap a piece of tape around that exact center spot, positioned so you can make your cut right in the center of the tape. Then, if you hold the two cords just as they are stacked and fold them in half again, tape around the center spots, and make the cuts, you would have four strands.

When you stack multiple strands to knot together, the outside strands usually need to run longer because they are making larger loop pathways than the inner strands. I also recommend that you estimate extra cord (a few inches per strand) for the hanging loop so you can choose to elongate the loop, and an equal amount (a few inches per strand) at the tail end below the last knot so you can fray the ends, attach tassels, or make a different cut after your piece is finished. You should factor in even more additional cord if you are making a chain of knots and would like cord space between the knots. Keep these things in mind when you are planning the length of cord you're cutting for your project and always generously overestimate your cord amount.

Cost

Often your projects are limited by your material budget, but don't be afraid of working under constraints. What may seem like a limitation is actually a creative challenge that is inviting you to dig deeper within yourself. Restrictions of resources or budget can often deflate creative newcomers who want to immediately work with their dream materials. When I reflect on the evolution of my own work, I see that working around those limitations shaped my unique jewelry aesthetic in ways that set me apart as an artist. When learning a new craft, it's important to have gratitude and excitement to learn the skill in whatever direction pans out and let go of some of the grander visions of what you could accomplish in the beginning. Even if you have the finest materials at your disposal as a beginner, as you become more experienced you may see your early learning phase as an unnecessary material cost because you couldn't yet accomplish the technique to serve the cost of the materials. Experiment to find alternatives and salvage free or low-cost materials from local creative depots, thrift stores, and swaps. Dive in wherever you are, keep your attitude curious and your mind open, and focus on building skills.

Color

Colors, like tastes, are powerful symbols that we link to our moods and personal experiences. The color choices in your creations can elevate, calm, energize, or inspire. Let's test your color sensitivity. Take some deep breaths, close your eyes, and visualize being drenched in the color plum as it fills the space around you and clothes you. Do any feelings arise? Now, feel the colorscape shift to a pale blue, noting any feelings that surface. Last, feel it shift a bright lemon yellow. Did you viscerally feel the difference in mood when the colors changed? If so, you are very receptive to color, which may add another layer of complexity and enjoyment to your creative process. Use color choices to boost, guide, or trigger a feeling you want to evoke within yourself while you are working creatively.

How will you choose your colors? For both a mood enhancer and as an overall aesthetic guide for your work, I recommend starting with a photograph or building an altar of objects that connect to the emotion you want to feel in your work. For example, if you are seeking a meditative calm, you may choose a photo of a watery landscape that gives you a relaxed feeling and then source the exact creams, blues, greens, and deep indigos to make your fiber necklace or bedroom wall hanging. Identify the main colors within the image and source the material colors from it by making swatches of the colors with markers on paper, paint chips collected from the hardware store, Pantone swatches online, or tiny yarn tassels mounted on a card that you can reference while shopping for your materials.

I have found that a few simple approaches to color pairings work best with knotted wall hangings and jewelry: neutral, monochromatic, contrasting, and rainbow.

Neutral: The neutral approach is just as it sounds and is the easiest, least expensive, and most accessible option for wall hangings. Select cords and yarns in various shades of cream, white, or tan, and you are ensured to have a piece that lends itself to a wide range of decor.

Monochromatic: For the monochromatic approach with non-neutrals, choose a main color and add colors a couple shades lighter and a couple shades darker to create your palette. This scheme works great for jewelry because the piece centers on a stunning color range within the same family, which makes it easy to pair with outfits. Start by choosing your cord in the main color; then, add yarn tassels in the lighter colors and gemstones in the darker shades. Experiment with mixing it up. For example, find a cord in the darkest shade, tassels in the main color, and a bead in the lightest color.

Contrasting: A contrasting color scheme involves choosing two opposing colors that harmonize and balance each other. Classic complementary color pairs include blue and orange, purple and yellow, and green and red. Don't feel you should take this too literally, as it relates to more than primary shades; you can use the complementary principle to pair black and white, soft lavender with a buttery yellow, or a gentle mint green with a deep dark scarlet. The contrast approach is eye-catching and ideal for jewelry.

Rainbow: A rainbow color-pairing theme is quite simple and great for wall hangings because it is an invitation for joy and playfulness to enter your space. Select five to ten colors using either the traditional ROYGBIV (red, orange, yellow, green, blue, indigo, violet) scheme or an assortment of your favorite tones. These colors may be represented across different embellishments that make up your piece, or they may be represented in one aspect such as a cascading rainbow of tassels, a chakra-like bead pattern in the center of your knots, or a stack of rainbow cords to knot.

If you want to develop a cohesive aesthetic within your creations, working with a single type of cord that offers an array of colors all within your ideal palette will help you develop a signature look. For a neutral palette, it will be quite easy for you to stick to the wide array of white, ecru, tan, and brown cords in cotton rope, jute, and hemp. If you are drawn to subtle pastel tones, you'll find your palette in plant- and animal-based materials such as felted wool cords, naturally dyed yarns, and single ply or twist cotton cords. For bright saturated colors, try cotton macramé twist rope or synthetics such as paracord, bungee cord, and polypropylene macramé cord. While mass-produced cords offer fewer color options than other materials, you can expand your palette through the embellishments you add to your cords and do-it-yourself cord treatments and techniques.

Color doesn't exist in a vacuum; your perceptions of a color can greatly change depending on what other colors are nearby. It's startling how a very bland blue cord can take on a whole new appeal when a contrasting amber stone is placed in the center of a blue knot. Embellishments such as beads, charms, gems, and yarn tassels with endless color options can enliven your knotted creations. But if finding specific cord colors is of primary importance, you may want to explore the next section on making your own cord.

MAKE YOUR OWN CORD

The recommended cord in most modern knotting books is typically manufactured in bland or primary and secondary color options, such as the standard red, blue, yellow, orange, purple, and so on. If you have trouble finding shades that inspire you, my suggestion is that you should experiment with making your own cord and surface treatments. Color is such an important guiding factor in my work that my journey to finding the right colors is completely responsible for my signature aesthetic. I could never find the range of colors in manufactured cording that I was envisioning for my creations. Poring over vintage fiber and jewelry

instructional books one day, I noticed something different: There were fewer design choices based on convenience and a lot more time-consuming, hands-on options. Funky do-it-yourself '70s jewelry books had tricks and techniques for producing your own cord. I tried braiding fibers into cord, knitting tubes of cord, and stuffing fiber tubes. I finally settled on thread wrapping rope to gain more control of cord diameter, texture, and color. Every technique comes with a list of pros and cons; it's just a question of which cons are less of a deal breaker for you personally. The major drawback for thread wrapping for me was the intense amount of labor involved, but having control over the other aspects of the process took precedence and I was motivated by the vision in my mind. I tried to mediate the drawback by finding a thick thread that would make the process go quicker.

As I began wrapping different internal structures—from a bumpy cotton braid rope to a smooth poly braid—the firmness and look of the cord changed, and so did the way it responded to knotting. The way your material responds to techniques will dramatically change not only the look of your work, but also the range of design options you have. Continuing to be flexible about my materials as I grow and evolve has been essential. When I started to experiment on a larger scale, wrapping got more difficult and exhausting with larger cord diameters. Sometimes, the techniques you use for one cord just won't have the same effect

on a cord in a different scale or material, so at times you have to be flexible to shift techniques.

I turned to dyeing when I started to explore cotton rope in larger diameters. I experimented with natural and synthetic dyes, eventually settling on Procion dyes for the saturation and color range that fit my aesthetic. I used large plastic storage containers for dye baths, following the standard fabric dyeing instructions and bundling the ropes into mesh laundry bags to prevent tangling before loading them in the washer for the final rinse. I preserved the color by hanging the ropes outside to air-dry on a sunny day rather than using a machine dryer. Most dyes adhere well to cotton but not to synthetics, so note your cord material when choosing a dye and monitor its time while in the dye bath; you may need to shorten or lengthen the time depending on how the cord absorbs the color. Your materials will reveal what they do best, so allow that discovery to be a driving force in developing your process and your overall aesthetic. The more unique your materials are, the more they express your personal creative journey.

PREPARING YOUR CORD FOR KNOTTING

The first step in preparing to knot is having the right cord length and diameter for what you envision making. Rope diameters are typically measured in inches and their lengths in feet. A bundle of rope is called a hank and is typically purchased in units of 10 feet, 25 feet, 50 feet, or 100 feet. Rope lengths longer than 100 feet are generally sold by the spool, making long lengths easier to unwind and store. Smaller varieties of cord, like those used for jewelry and upholstery, are measured for length by the foot, yard, or meter and for diameter by millimeters. They are sold in bundles or on spools. I recommend these three lengths and varieties for personal knot practice:

- 50 feet ¼-inch cotton braid rope
- 25–50 feet 3 mm or 4 mm 550 paracord
- 2–4 mm satin rattail at 20–100 yards depending on your budget and desire

Length estimation can get tricky until you know your personal knotting style. Some people like their knots compact, while others, like myself, prefer a lot of open space within the knot and between the knots. In my wall-hanging workshops, students typically created 18-inch to 36-inch knotted wall art using 50 feet of ⅜-inch-diameter cotton braid rope. Usually, they had some excess rope left over—sometimes even enough to make a small piece. It's rare not to have leftover cord because the process of making the knots requires a lot of space before the knot is tightened. Once the knot is tightened, the excess that helped you to comfortably manipulate the shape is then pushed out of the design leaving longer ends that then can be trimmed to the right proportion. The less slack you leave yourself to knot, the more difficult it is, so I always work big and then tighten accordingly and cut the excess at the end.

I suggest intentionally overestimating the amount of cord needed for new projects for three reasons: to encourage you to work big while you are following the diagrams; to accommodate any additional strands, knots, or negative space you want to weave in; and to allow you more slack for the last knot in a sequence. When working with finer cords, add even more length so you can better see what you are working on and more easily manipulate thin or slippery cords. As you become a more proficient knotter, you can become more efficient with your cordage, estimate length more accurately, and use less than the amounts I recommend with these projects. To summarize, the amount of cord you need for a personal project depends on these factors:

- Diameter of the cord
- Which knots you are making
- How loose or tight your knotting style is
- How many strands you are stacking to create the knot

When in doubt, overestimate the length!

To estimate cord length for a project or to practice designs before committing to premium materials, I recommend prototyping the design with less expensive, more common cords. While knotting is a very forgiving craft, buying too much, buying too little, or cutting the wrong lengths can cost you time, money, or scarce materials. Materials such as silk cord and felted wool can sometimes develop creasing from being repeatedly knotted or sewn, and it can be hard to return the cord to its pristine state. Stuffed fabric tubes may look sturdier but can retain dents and bumps from previous ties. A good solution is to keep some cords handy to use and reuse for prototypes so you avoid wearing down fancier cords.

Get the closest prototype cord for the most accurate estimation by choosing one that is a similar diameter and density. Poly rope from the hardware store is a great cord to have on hand for prototyping larger designs because it can be used infinitely and is very inexpensive. For small projects, paracord is ideal for prototyping. Having a little more material on hand than the exact amount required is also helpful; you may need more or less cord depending on how much slack you like while knotting and how much negative space you like within your knots.

A guideline in macramé is that you need about three to four times the length you want your finished piece to be; however, the mat knot designs in this book are a different story. They involve too many factors that determine length to give a simple calculation or a rough estimate. For project estimation, I always keep old cords in different diameters so I can prototype the rough design in a cord of similar texture and diameter and then undo the design and measure the rope I used; I usually add about one-third additional length as a safety measure. The only thing you need to be really hesitant about in knotting is making a cut—once the cut is made, the sections usually can't be reattached.

When you have determined the length and you are ready to cut a strand off a spool or hank, measure the cord and wrap a piece of masking tape or scotch tape around the cord at the spot where you'll make the cut. Then, using a sharp pair of scissors, make a clean cut through the center of the taped section, leaving half the taped section around the end of your strand and the other half on the spool or hank. These pieces of tape will keep the cord ends from fraying when cut and from unraveling while knotting. You'd be surprised how much length you can lose to fraying and unraveling if you don't tape the ends. To keep the ends crisp while you knot and sew, remove the tape as the very last step of your project.

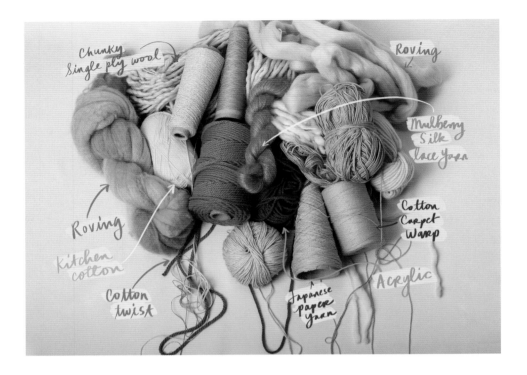

Yarn

If you plan on incorporating wrapping or tassel making into your practice, yarn will be an important part of your material search. Yarn brings more color and texture into a knotted piece, which expands the palette to explore. Similar to cording, yarn can vary by texture, budget, material, and so on. See page 25 for more on yarn.

Fiber Practice Journal

The best place to record your materials and experiments is in a fiber journal. For a do-it-yourself approach, fill a standard academic binder with hole-punched, cardstock pages mounted to cardboard to make sure the pages don't buckle as you attach materials to them. Or, you can purchase an artist presentation book (try brands such as Blick, Itoya, or Prat), which is a spiral binder filled with clear, refillable poly pockets with a blank page in each to keep your attached pieces secure and hold loose materials. I use a big landscape portfolio that measures 11 by 17 inches from Blick Art Materials. Pages can be cycled in and out of the book and new pages can be purchased separately. Fix material samples to your paper sheets by using museum wax, superglue, staples, pins, hand-sewn stitches through the paper, or tape. You may want to start your journal by creating a color palette of collected materials that inspire you. These materials may be bits and pieces of anything that catches your eye: strands of yarn, fabric swatches, a collage of images from books and magazines, personal photos, hardware store paint chips, swaths of fabric, or paint or colored pencil (see pages 11–14 for color and 13 for using image references). As you begin to practice and purchase materials, note the following information in your journal:

- Material descriptor
- Color (the official descriptor given by the manufacturer)
- Source (where it was purchased)
- Price x size/length = cost per unit
- Notes on technique applications

In my early experiments in jewelry, I kept all my strange little sections and snippets of fiber experiments taped, glued, and pinned into a binder. It allowed me to contrast and compare how different materials responded to different techniques and to easily source materials I had purchased in the past. As I worked, I taped 3-inch sections of each cord and yarn piece I had used with notes in the margin on the brand, color, cord diameter, cost per foot, location purchased, material, and general observations about working with it: Does it kink when twisted or braided? Does it have "memory" or mold? Does it hold shapes easily? Does the color vary wildly from batch to batch? Experimental knotted or sewn sections that are small and flat can also be pinned, glued, or taped into the journal. A journal keeps a record of your material purchases, budget, and knotting journey, is a handy reference for future designs, and becomes a beautiful book of your progress in the medium.

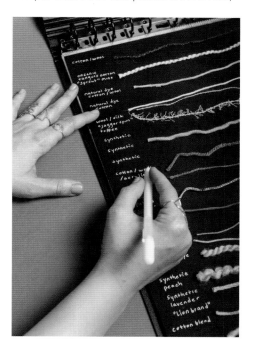

matching thread

needle

pins

tape measure

mat surface

Rope or cord

tape for securing rope ends

comb for tassels

scissors

yarn for tassels

Gathering Your Tools

To knot, all you absolutely need is cord, but a few handy tools can make knotting easier, expand your creative skill set, and offer you more design options.

Knot Board: A knot board is not essential, but it is helpful when using finer cording, making intricate knots, and protecting your work surface if you like to pin as you go. If you are envisioning knotting while sitting on a couch or making projects with fine cording, you should make or purchase one. Macramé boards can be purchased in craft stores, or French Memo Boards or a piece of foam core can be used as makeshift knot boards. I have a small French Memo Board near my bed for nighttime knotting, which works perfectly for making small knots on my lap. However, the most comfortable variety would probably be something from the do-it-yourself category.

Here's one idea for an easy, inexpensive knot board that you can make from simple materials. Take a firm board in a square or rectangular size that would feel most comfortable in your lap; generally 11 to 20 inches wide and 14 to 26 inches long is adequate. The board could be bigger, like a drawing board, if you envision leaning it against a desk or table as you sit in your chair. It could also be smaller, like the size of a dinner tray, if you want to lay it across your lap or prop it against your bent legs while semi-reclining in bed. Cover the board with a layer of cushion to sink your pins into. The cushion could be a layer or two of corkboard glued or stapled to the board or thick foam batting with fabric stretched over the top and stapled to the back. Whatever your pins can sink into sturdily will be fine.

To use the board, stick a pin through the cord and into the board wherever you need reinforcement to hold a shape you have formed in place. A knot board not only helps you to keep cord sections in the proper shapes, but it also allows you to leave your work intact so you can continue later.

Scissors: It's probably obvious that if you want to cut your cord into multiple strands or determine the exact length of your finished piece, you'll need scissors. Find a nice sharp pair that makes a clean, crisp cut. Of course, any old pair of scissors will do, but you'll marvel at the clean cord ends after using extra-sharp shears. A pair of scissors from your local fabric store will do nicely, but only use them for paper, fabric, cord, and other fibrous things or the blades will dull more quickly.

Tape: If you first tape around the circumference of your cord at the cutting spot with a soft tape such as masking tape or scotch tape, and then make the cut at the center of the taped section, you will get a much cleaner cut and the ends of your cord won't unravel while you work. It's shocking to see how many inches of your rope ends you can lose while you are working with untaped ends that naturally fray and untwist or unbraid as the rope is being worked. When your piece is finished, you can finally remove the bits of tape on your cord ends and still have freshly cut endings on your piece. If you are working with a rough rope such as jute or manila rope, taping your fingers with medical tape will help protect your skin from becoming chafed. (If you are working with a large quantity of rough rope or have sensitive skin, choose gloves instead.)

Pins: Pinning your cords together or to the board is a helpful way to make intricate shapes and work with multiple layered strands. As you work through a diagram, it is essential that the negative spaces and line shapes of the cord follow those of the step-by-step you are working on. After each step, check the design to see if your work-in-progress matches the picture of the last step you completed. Reason being, as you continue to work the cord ends, the cord has a tendency to pull the shapes you have already made out of proportion. If the diagram is instructing you to insert a cord end into a loop and the correct loop on your work-in-progress is distorted, too small, or too big, you could mistake another area for the correct one and insert your rope into the wrong place. One small mistake like that can render a knot saggy and an altogether confusing tangle. For that reason and more, it's a good idea to use pins to anchor the shapes you are making as you work. That means placing a pin through each cord intersection and into the board so it stays in place.

Students always wonder if there's a science to pinning; there is not! It's all personal preference. Some people like to pin generously, and others barely use them at all. Start by just placing pins at cord intersections and on loose shapes in progress—essentially anywhere proportions could become easily distorted. A pin is not set in stone though; remember that you may need to remove pins as you work different areas to pick up slack and to prevent or allow cord movement as necessary. A board and pins aren't absolute requirements for knotting, but if you're a beginner or are challenged by any of the knots, these tools do wonders for your process.

Needle and Thread: Sewing is always the last step in creating knot designs. For the majority of decoration or jewelry designs, you will need to do at least a minimal amount of sewing when the design is completed if you want to hang the design on the wall or make a wearable item. Find a needle that is suited to your cording; the finer the cording is, the finer the needle should be. Just about any needle works, but certain needles can make your work a lot easier and a lot faster.

- For crochet thread or yarn, use a tapestry or chenille needle for its large eye.
- To sew across large-diameter ropes, try soft sculpture needles or darning needles.
- If you are dealing with thick, solid rope that is hard to sew through, try sharps, betweens, or quilting needles, which have very fine points and slip into the crevices more easily.
- For fine, delicate cord, try beading needles, which are ultra-fine and slip through the cord without tearing a conspicuous hole.
- To make tassels, use a tapestry needle.

If you're still having trouble sewing through your cord, which can require a lot of hand strength, I advise a small pair of jewelry pliers to help pull the needle out at the end of each stitch. Using a thread that closely matches the color of the cord will go a long way toward disguising less-than-perfect stitches.

Yarn: If you want to make tassels or experiment with weaving or wrapping, I highly advise picking up a few skeins of yarn that catch your eye. A vast array of yarn is available in gorgeous colors from hand-dyed, small batches from natural sources that vary subtly to super pigmented, mass-produced synthetics. Rather than go to the big-box chain stores, check out your local mom-and-pop yarn store. Local shop staff tend to know yarn to the T because they are staffed by experienced crafters who are great sounding boards, and they may even call company representatives for you if they can't answer specific questions. Yarns run the gamut from super fuzzy with a halo of frizz around each strand to tight, compact "kitchen cottons" that were traditionally used to make potholders and dish towels with minimal fuzz. What look you're going for will depend on the textural aspects of the yarn, the material it is composed of, and the color. Experiment, experiment, experiment.

Superglue: Some people fancy finished pieces with raw cord ends rather than disguising them with tassels as I tend to do. In that case, a touch of clear glue will secure freshly cut cord ends to keep them from unraveling.

Soft tape measure: A flexible measuring tape (like a tailor uses) is very helpful in determining how much cording you need for a particular project. For example, if you are debating after the fact if you should layer in or stack your cord so it is doubled, you might want to measure the cord in the design as it has currently been made. To do so, simply wind the tape measure along the cord's loops and curves instead of undoing or remaking the whole design. Once you've measured, you have a gauge for how much more cord you will need and can check your supply to make sure you have enough, or you can record the information in your fiber journal so you know how much of that particular cord you will need for a future project. Remember, different cord diameters require different lengths of cord to make the same designs.

Awl/crochet hook: If you are using thin cord that is finer than 6 millimeters, an awl, tweezers, or crochet hook can help you to untangle or undo knots with ease.

Beads and charms: You may want to sew beads, gemstones, or metal charms in the negative space between cords or on the cord itself. You can search for the right charm after the fiber part of your piece is finished, or you can pick out a stone and work around it. Either way, it can be helpful to have a few charms on hand to experiment with.

Preparing to Knot

Gather your supplies and get comfortable at a large table or on the floor. As a beginner, it will be easier to knot in a quiet environment where you can focus. If you are just knotting for fun or experimentation, the supplies I would suggest are scissors, the rope/cord, a knotting board, and pins. If you're sitting at the table, the easiest position to work from is to balance a large knotting board on your lap and lean it against the table so it slants like an easel. A small knot board isn't as useful for large wall hangings, but it can also be positioned at a slant if you lay it on the table and stack books or other objects under the side farthest away from you. If you are working with thick rope, ³/₈-inch diameter or larger, or if you're working with 25 feet or more as we do in my knot workshop, you may find sitting on the floor a lot easier. If you're pinning your cord sections on the floor and not using the board, take care to avoid the pins when you grab the backside of your work (speaking from lots of experience here). As your skills grow, you will easily be able to make all of the simple knots in this book without the aid of pins or a knot board.

Plan your design in advance to know what length cord you will need. Of course, the thickness of the cord you use, how loose or tight you choose to make each knot, and the number of strands you use will cause the cord length to vary.

I recommend knotting different styles and sizes of cords. Try each knot out using a generous scrap of your desired cord, and after completing the knot, measure how much you used for each style and size so you can better plan the length of cord you need for your wall hanging. To measure cord, either (1) tie a knot and tighten it until it's perfect, then untie it and measure the length of cord with a ruler, or (2) tie a knot and use a soft tape measure to trace each strand of cord along the knot, recording the lengths. Work through each of the knots and record in your fiber practice journal (see page 132) the lengths necessary to make each knot.

A GUIDE TO KNOTTING

Whether you intend to follow a traditional knotting practice or invent your own unique knots, understanding the mechanics of knotting will help you do both. As you work through the diagrams, you will intuitively begin to get a feel for what holds a knot together, so to speak. This section is essentially a guide to understanding the anatomy of a knot, how knots vary, and how they work. As you progress to complete a traditional knot or design a vision you have, refer back to this section for guidance.

The Knotting Process

Every knot flows through three basic phases: weaving, tightening, and finishing.

WEAVING

As you work through the knot diagrams, you will find they comprise steps for weaving Strands A and B over and under one another. Each step contains an arrow, showing the weaving motion in the color of the cord performing the motion. Only one cord per step is the "working end"; in other words, in each step, one cord is stationary and one is performing the movement (the working end). The intersection of Strands A and B creates the tension and support that allow the knot to take shape. Pay close attention to which cord goes under and which goes over at each intersection because this is crucial to your knot being completed correctly. After you have completed the weaving motion directed by the arrow's path, check each cord intersection on your knot against the diagram to ensure the correct cord is over or under before you move on to the next step. The simplest mistake of weaving the cord over when you should have gone under can cause your knot to collapse or transform into the wrong design.

If you finish weaving and realize something went wrong, don't attempt to perform a CSI autopsy investigation on your failed knot; just untie it and start again! Most beginners have the feeling that they need to find the mistake and salvage the correct work they've invested into it. Inevitably, this attempt usually leaves students feeling more confused, tired, and annoyed after spending 20 minutes trying to figure out the mistake when instead they could have tied the knot over from the beginning faster and gained a better grasp of the knot. One of the great advantages knotting has over other crafts is that knotting is a very forgiving medium. If you are working with a utilitarian cord like rope or paracord, you can do and undo your work endless times.

TIGHTENING

Believe it or not, even after all the steps of the knot are correctly completed, your knot may not yet resemble the final knot design. This is where the very important step of tightening comes in. How you tighten your knots will affect the overall aesthetic of your work, and how loose or tight your knots are can be personal preference. Tighten your shapes slowly and little by little. Start at the top of one side first (either A or B) where the cord enters the knot (or from the hanging loop if it is your only knot on that cord) and follow the strand's pathway, easing out kinks and moving the slack down the knot and out through the exit cord. Repeat the same smoothing process on the other strand. You may need to repeat this entire process several times. With each round of tightening, the knot gains proportion and becomes more compact.

Often knot diagrams are woven correctly in the first step but are tightened incorrectly. When one area is loosened or overtightened, proportions are thrown off and cause the knot to appear incorrectly tied when it was not. Avoid yanking a cord section while tightening because this action throws the knot out of proportion and can result in a tangled lump. With practice, you will better understand how to tighten. Remember: (1) Always start on one side only—either A or B—at the entry point/hanging loop and work your way all the way down through the exit point before addressing the other side; (2) go slow, gently tightening little by little; and (3) keep an eye on your proportions, shaping and maintaining the same proportions of the diagram as you go.

FINISHING

In the last step, complete your knot by sewing its anchor points and any beads, charms, or tassels in place and by finishing off the cord ends in the style of your preference. Ensure your work is woven and tightened to perfection before finishing, because once stitches are made, your design is locked into place. Any problems you want to fix after the knot has been stitched will require ripping out stitches throughout the piece. Removing stitches from rope can usually be done without any trace, but removing stitches from fine cording can cause irreparable damage to the cord. After you have added embellishments and sewn your design into place, polish off the cord ends by hiding them with tassels, fraying them to create a pretty fringe, dabbing them with clear glue, burning the ends (to melt and seal the ends of synthetic cords), or simply trimming them to a neat edge. More extensive directions on finishing are located on pages 61–63 (anchor stitches) and pages 63–73 (beads and tassels).

knot sequence wallhanging anatomy

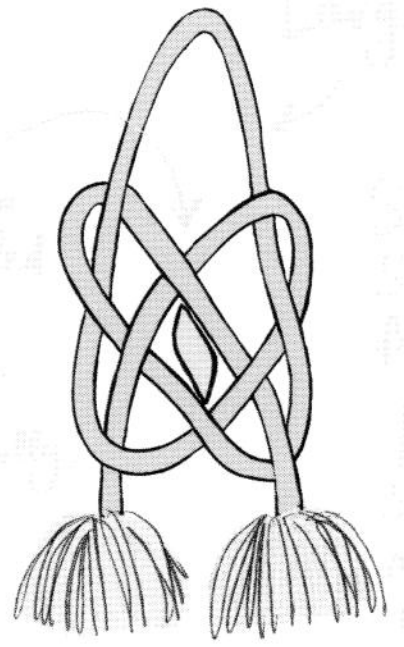

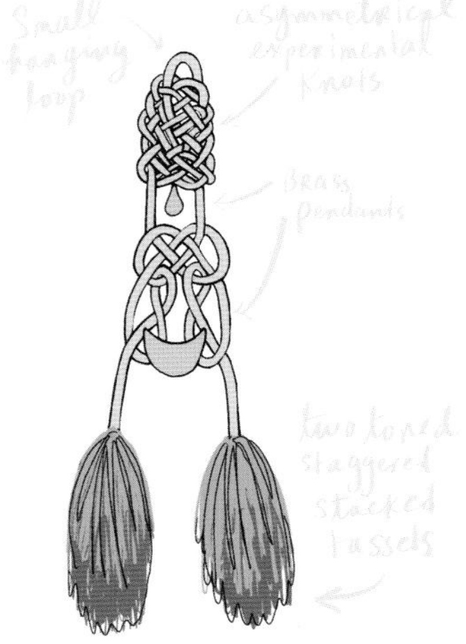

Large hanging loop

entire Ribbon

Single Sailor's breastplate

Requires sewing for mounting hanging negative space

Small hanging loop

asymmetrical experimental knots

brass pendants

two toned staggered stacked tassels

Center of entire Rope strand

hanging loop

Bead

Sailor's Breastplate

double coin

BRASS Charm

Weaver's plait

windows

Square knot

free style tassels

Bead

Sew sturdy anchor stitches to have large "windows" of negative space between knots

tassels for proportion & balance

gather cord ends into a single knot

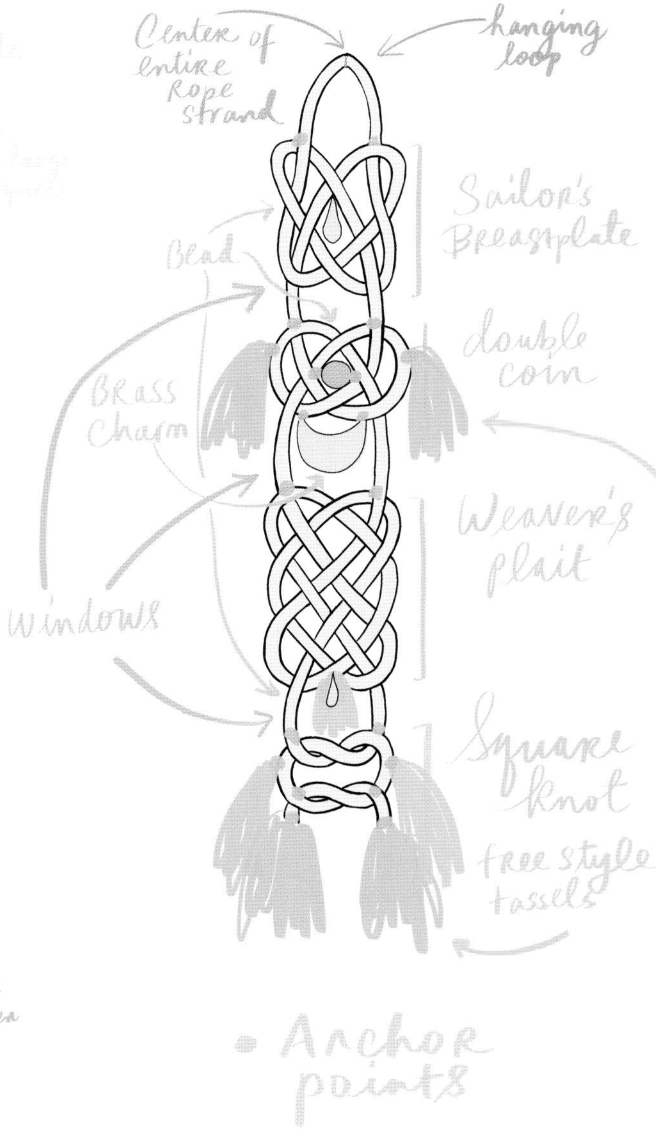

Anchor points

KNOTTING TERMS

Anchor Knot: A very sturdy, tight knot that helps a knot chain maintain its shape. Some good examples of anchor knots are the Double Connection, Clasped Hands, and Cross Knot. These knots are great to begin and end a vertical knot chain wall hanging or to scatter throughout a piece to anchor some of the loose knots.

Anchoring/Anchor Stitch: After your wall hanging or necklace is complete, you will use these stitches, hidden in the spaces where the cords overlap, to maintain the shape of the knot.

Butterfly/Figure 8 Cord Bundle: A way to keep long cord ends neat as you work with thinner cords such as rattail and paracord, this bundle can be formed with your excess cord by swirling it between your thumb and pinky in a figure 8 shape and tying it off with a rubber band. As you work that line of cord, you can gradually release slack from the bundle.

Cord Intersection: Any point where the cord strands overlap in the over-under pattern is called a cord intersection.

Entry Points/Exit Points: The entry points are just above the cord intersections where the rope strands enter the top of the knot. The exit points are just below the cord intersections where the cord flows out of the knot. In other words, these points are the areas where each strand enters or exits the knot. All the knots in this book have two entry points and two exit points.

Finishing: Finishing makes a knot sturdy, permanent, and decorative by sewing stitches in certain places to bind it together and/or by embellishing it with final touches.

Hanging Loop: A folded construction wall hanging or sculptural knot is hung from this loop.

Hitch: This variety of knot uses a continuous loop to connect rope to another object. In design and ornamentation, hitches are most commonly used in macramé to attach ropes to a bar. The ropes will be knotted to form a panel, and the bar can then be hung from a wall or ceiling.

Mat Knot: Also called flat knot. This type of knot is flat and woven. In this book, the Weaver's Plait, Sailor's Breastplate, Double Coin, Sun Cycle, and Cloud Knot are all mat knots. Mat knots are best for wall hangings, rugs, and surface accents due to their flat, two-dimensional characteristics.

Tail: The cords that exit a knot and hang loosely out the bottom of the knot are called tails. Tails are usually trimmed to a shorter, more even length as a very last step in finishing a wall hanging.

Tightening: This final stage shapes and shrinks intricate knots with even pressure applied from the starting point of each strand to its end. Through tightening, your knot becomes firm, smooth, and proportioned.

Vertical Knot Chain: A sequence of knots that are created to flow in a straight line from top to bottom. Knots with two entry points and two exit points can simply be incorporated into a vertical knot chain. This is the type of wall hanging demonstrated in this book, and each knot except the Pipa Knot can be incorporated into a vertical knot chain.

Weaving: Also known as tying, this over-under movement of the cord creates a knot.

Working End: The cord end in each step of the diagram that is currently performing the weaving motion is called the working end. In every diagram up to the tightening step, either Strand A or Strand B will be the working end.

top to
bottom
construction

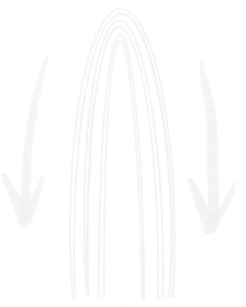

folded
construction

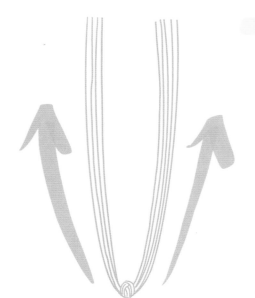

Symmetrical
Construction

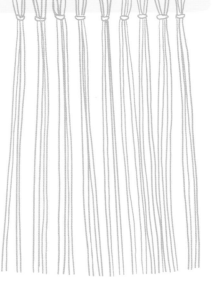

Panel
Construction

Methods of Construction

The kind of project you plan to work on will determine the method of construction you choose. In this book, we will only use two of the four modes of construction: folded construction and panel construction.

TOP TO BOTTOM CONSTRUCTION

In this construction, you align the parallel cord strands and work vertically from one end to the other. Although this type of construction isn't demonstrated in this book, it is an important construction style because it is the first type of knot construction most people learn as children (think friendship bracelets) and it illustrates another potential option for lining up cords for knotting.

FOLDED CONSTRUCTION

Variations of the folded construction method are used for most of the knots and projects in this book. For this construction, you are folding a length of cord in half and using the center point as the top of your piece, allowing the right and left sides to hang down loosely from the center peak, as if you're outlining a mountain. This method is an easy way to create things that hang on the wall. It is often used to make bracelets because you fold the cord in half, creating a loop that can double as a fastener. The loop is also a perfect point from which to hang your work on the wall.

SYMMETRICAL CONSTRUCTION

The symmetrical construction is a method for creating simple pendant necklaces, commonly used when the pendant is a metal or bead charm placed at the center. Instead of beginning from a curve with the peak of the mountain at the top as in folded construction, the curve in symmetrical construction is flipped so its center is at the bottom and the cord ends are at the top. Just as you would with the folded construction, begin from the center of the folded curve, but this time you are working from the bottom and up the sides of the necklace toward the clasp. After adding a pendant, work continues separately along Strands A and B, as you knot or add other embellishments. The clasps are added last.

PANEL CONSTRUCTION

As the basis of macramé, panel construction allows you to create textile-like two-dimensional surfaces. By hitching strands of rope from a bar, pipe, dowel, rod, or cord, you can weave the strands together with simple knots, hitches, or half-hitches. A simple alternation of the knot designs by row and column leads to beautiful patterns in the panel. Generally, with this mode of construction, you are working from left to right or right to left to create rows of knots across the vertically hanging ropes. The Double Coin Curtain project on page 110 utilizes this mode of construction.

The Principles of Knotting

Finally, with the basic process down, I think about several additional elements when I work: tension, space, style, and play.

BALANCED TENSION

Balanced tension is essential to making a knot hold its shape—especially if your design has significant negative space within it. Symmetry in the tension doesn't have to mean symmetry in the shape of the knot. Even abstract, asymmetrical design knots have ingenious ways to balance tension. Whether symmetrical or asymmetrical, when the tension of the rope is balanced, the knot often looks balanced to the eye as well. You'll know something isn't quite right with your knot if it leans heavily to one side, comes loose, and/or feels floppy.

SPACE IS THE PLACE

One of the great contradictions of knotting is that you create space in the tightening step. Tightening is as much about balancing the negative space in a design as it is about making sure the cord pathways are taut. Knots take on many disguises during the process, sometimes looking unrecognizable from one form to the next depending on how the knotter increases and decreases space within the loops. Spacing within the knot can be used to alter or distort the proportions of the knot (for example, increasing the size of the outer loops or shrinking them versus increasing the size of negative space in the center loop of the knot)

or to create original, new designs. This is a fun element to play with. A knot comprises both the negative space and the linework created by the cord.

THE BEST STYLE IS NO STYLE

Some of the most interesting knots are created by fusing steps of different knots together, looping in new cords, or building off the traditional knots in new directions. Research further into the cultural knot traditions mentioned in this book to see what they offer, and then let loose. Don't feel constrained to tradition; the pioneers of knotting are those who created their own designs to solve problems in their daily life or to develop aesthetically imaginative shapes. Focusing too intently on imitating a certain style can cause you to inhibit your own creativity or establish a rigid knotting practice.

GREAT WORK IS PLAY

The more you play and experiment outside of the set diagrams, the more exciting ideas will arise and the more your aesthetic will develop. Get yourself into tricky situations and challenge yourself to work through them. Experiment with adding a few extra loops to a traditional knot you've mastered. How does it change the shape? Is the tension still balanced throughout the knot? If not, how can you alter it or add more loops to the shape to achieve a balanced tension?

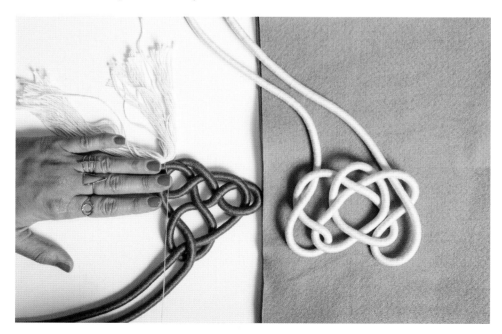

BASIC KNOTS

The knots in this section are some essentials for your beginner's toolkit and all you need to complete the projects in this book. A description of the knot's origins and its symbolic meanings is included with each knot. See page 137 for the challenging Pan Chang Knot. Other popular knots that you may want to check out but aren't included here are Monkey's Fist, Butterfly Knot, Good Luck Knot, Ring of Coins Knot, and Star Knot.

How to Read Knot Diagrams

The knot diagrams in this book aren't difficult to grasp, but getting the hang of reading diagrams can feel like deciphering another language. Once you understand the logic of how diagrams function, then you can read them fluently from book to book. I like to offer instructions based on diagram drawings instead of photos or videos because diagrams are the age-old, universal method for communicating knotting. If you are empowered to read knot diagrams, you can knot with ease from an old sailor's book as well as know how to draw diagrams to record your own knot designs.

All of the knots and projects in this book use the folded construction method except the Double Coin Curtain. To begin any project using the folded construction method, take your cord (or cords if you are using multiple strands), fold them in half, and lay them in front of you in a bell curve with the peak of the hill at the top and the two ends cascading down. The peak of the hill, or center point of your cord, will become a hanging loop at the top of your piece. For each diagram, I've given the two working legs of the cord a different color, starting at the center point, and I've labeled these sides "A" and "B"; these markings are used to better show the knotting steps. Remember, only one strand is the working end per step. See the weaving section on page 28 for more information.

Part of what makes the style of knotting in this book versatile and appealing is that each knot, with the exception of the Pipa Knot (see page 58), can be tied in a vertical knot chain style (see page 33) because each has two entry points and two exit points allowing one knot to connect to another. As the two sides of your cord, A and B, are exiting your knot design, they are then picked up again to begin the entry points for the next knot that will sit below your last. You could potentially make an endless chain of every knot with two entry points and two exit points if you have enough cord. The diagrams are made as if you are making your first knot from the start of the hanging loop. This is significant, because once the first knot is made, the subsequent knots will no longer be made under the hanging loop shown in the diagrams but will be tied from two parallel cords that exit from the knot above. When looking at the diagram to make your subsequent knots on the chain, just ignore the hanging loop at the top. If it helps, cover up the loop part of the drawing with a piece of paper so you will be looking at what appears to be two parallel cords.

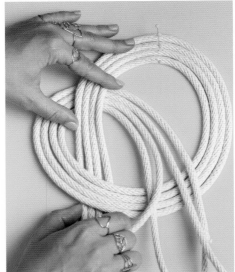

SQUARE KNOT

The Square Knot is the most widely known and utilized knot of them all. Used by everyone from scouts to sailors to macramé artists, the Square Knot ranges from utilitarian to decorative. It is known for universality, strength, utility, and balance. By switching the order in which you overlap the cords, you can change the pattern so it is leaning left, leaning right, or facing forward. This subtle shift between the overlap order of the knot is the most essential element in macramé design, which is commonly made with four cords: two outer cords knotted around two inner cords that fall straight through the center. You can create endless design variations through pattern and cord color with this simple knot, inspiring wild imagination through this grounded knot meditation.

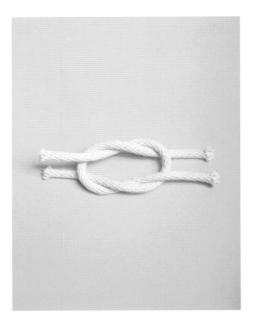
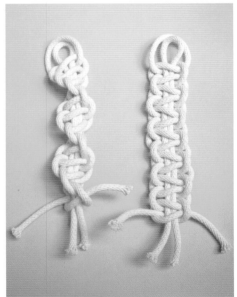

Square knot

Right Square

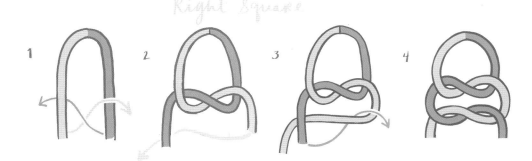

1　　2　　3　　4

Right Square Chain

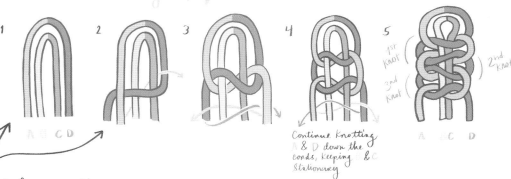

1　2　3　4　5

A B C D　　A B C D

4. Continue knotting A & D down the cords, keeping B & C stationary

5. 1st knot, 2nd knot, 2nd knot

A B C D

When creating a square chain, make the outer strands of the chain about three times longer to accommodate the wider pathway

To create a left square chain, switch the order in which the cords are overlapping for each diagram

To make a spiraling square chain, repeat just the first two steps down the chain, alternating A & D in the overlap. This is called a half square spiral in macramé

Spiral Square chain

or half square spiral chain

Left Square chain

DOUBLE COIN

PROSPERITY, WEALTH

Mysteriously, a few cultures around the world developed this same knot, attaching different names, usages, and value to it. We do not know if this design overlap is the result of intercultural copying, sharing, or simply an inevitable discovery that results from intertwining cords. This knot is referred to as the Carrick Bend (a practical knot in mariner culture) and the Josephine Knot (a decorative knot in Europe). In European cultures, it represents love, longing, and desire because the shape resembles the merging or embrace of two entities. Lore about the Josephine Knot's origin notes claims that sailors tied it as a visual representation of the mythology of Napoleon and Josephine's love affair and the lover they left on the shore. My personal preference for the conceptualization of this knot originates in China, where the design was thought to mimic two overlapping coins, helping its maker or owner manifest wealth and prosperity. As you gaze on this knot, the two coins may not be immediately apparent, but as you meditate on its linking coin shapes, be reminded of the abundance that we can feel by shifting our perspective on things around us.

The Double Coin will play an important role in your knot vocabulary because it is the basis of more complex, beautiful knots. While it is simple enough for beginners, it is also challenging enough to encapsulate the essence of knotting and offers so much potential for variation. You will quickly advance your knot skills by simply practicing this knot until it is intuitive and you no longer have to look at the diagram. Try creating an endless chain where one flows into the next and you will certainly absorb the foundational principles of knotting through that practice.

double coin

1

loop A under
itself & lay
over the
top of it

2

Make a loop
with that
weaves through
the loops

3

Note that loop "2"
is the hanging
loop

When the double
coin you're
making isn't the
first knot under
the hanging loop,
or is made from
two parallel cords,
this second step
will look like
this

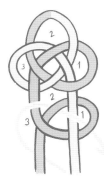

When you make
subsequent double
coins on a vertical
knot chain, the
"2" loop will
appear like
negative space
or a window
between knots

CROSS KNOT

While most knots are symmetrical from front to back, this knot magically displays two totally different designs: one side shows a cross; the other, a square or, some might say, the top of a hot cross bun or a king's crown. This double-sided nature offers a metaphorical glimpse at the mystery, power of transformation, and illusion of the universe. The historical intention of the knot, as with many knots, is difficult to trace, as it was likely developed before written records. Knot historian Lydia Chen reports its place of origin as China during the Tang and Song dynasties, which could put its development as early as 618 C.E., and notes that a cross conveys "10" in China, a number of wholeness, fullness, and perfection in numerology. Other sources claim its origin is in Japan, and the square side, as the front of the knot, symbolizes a crown. It is sometimes referred to in the West as the Friendship Knot, the Japanese Square Knot, the Chinese Cross Knot, and the Crown Knot. American Boy Scouts and Girl Scouts historically used the knot to tie their neck scarves to symbolize unity.

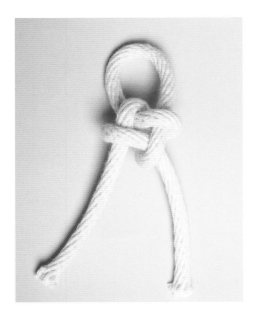 

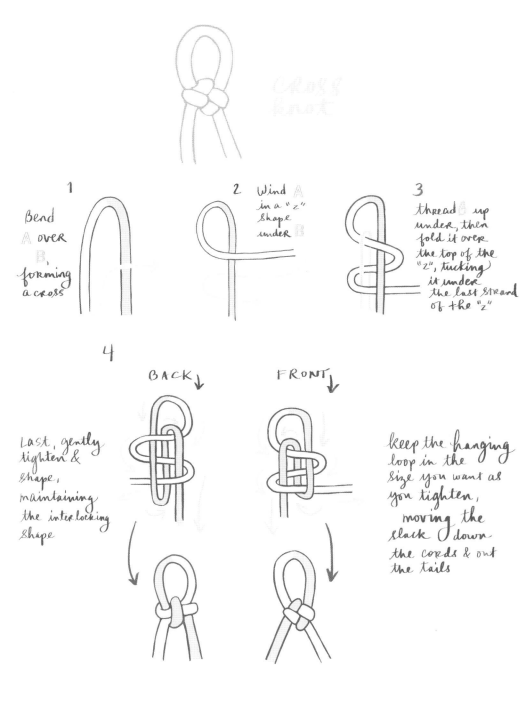

CROSS KNOT

1 Bend A over B, forming a cross

2 Wind in a "z" shape under

3 thread B up under, then fold it over the top of the "z", tucking it under the last strand of the "z"

4

BACK ↓

FRONT ↓

Last, gently tighten & shape, maintaining the interlocking shape

keep the hanging loop in the size you want as you tighten, moving the slack down the cords & out the tails

the back will form a cross shape and the front will form a hot cross bun shape

SUN CYCLE

LIFE CYCLES, COMPLETION, BEGINNING

Containing several interlocking rings, the Sun Cycle Knot looks as though it is documenting the cycle of the rising and setting sun. If you feel you have just completed a project, role, event, or relationship and are embarking on a new beginning, this knot is a perfect visual representation of that shift. Look at the pattern closely, and you'll see a knot you've already learned embedded within: essentially, this encircling pattern is an expanded-upon version of the Double Coin. I have noticed this knot and its many variations unnamed in historical sailor's books, likely because many versions can be created by building loops off of the main shape, experimenting with cord overlapping order, and exiting the cord ends through various points. Shared here are two different variations on this knot. More complex iterations include the Turtle Knot from Japan and the Ring of Coins developed by J. D. Lenzen. The Sun Cycle shows the potential of knotting—when you learn the fundamentals you can use them as building blocks to create new designs.

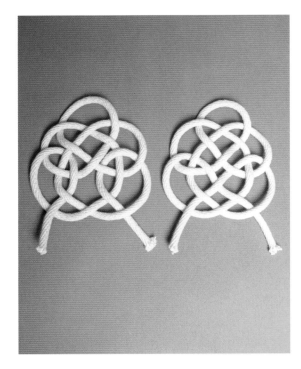

Sun Cycles

Create a loop with, winding the cord under itself

1

2

lay on top of the loop

3

Now make a loop with weaving it through the loop. Note that although it looks like a double coin, it has a different weaving pattern

4

this shape is floppy & needs to be locked down by the last two loops. Add the first by looping around to the left side

5

6

Create the next loop by looping around to the right & weaving diagonally through the knot back to the left side

4

this shape is floppy & needs to be locked down by the last two loops. loop to the left, weaving under

5

6

next, loop around to the right side weaving it through the knot & back down

SAILOR'S BREASTPLATE

STRUCTURE, PROTECTION

I originally found this knot in an out-of-print sailor's fancy knotwork manual from the early twentieth century. The striking shield design holds firmly even as a loose weave with lots of negative space. Alternatively, this knot is also referred to as a Celtic Square Knot. While its lovely, open-weave shape looks impressive, this knot is one of the simpler designs to master. I love the idea of the protective breastplate interpretation for the sailor and the softly woven square design from Celtic culture. The overlap between the box and the breastplate concepts seems to be the protective, comforting security of that gentle architecture.

Sailor's
Breastplate

1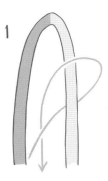

loop A around B from back to front

2

tuck B up through the loop A

3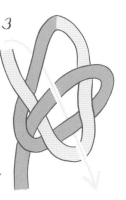

loop B back around A & weave back down through the knot diagonally

4

tighten & shape the proportions

CLOUD KNOT

LEVITY, SPIRITUAL TRANSCENDENCE

This knot can be seen in old sailor's knotting books as well as within the mass-produced, Chinese-style knotted wall hangings that were popular in the '70s and '80s. I have not been able to find a source that named or offered an origin story for this knot. It looks like a cloud to my eyes, which is a symbol of lightness, of being through sun and storm. One of the paradoxes represented by this knot is that clouds are light but take up a lot of space. The Cloud Knot is complex in appearance yet deceptively simple in construction. The contradiction in this knot evokes the Buddhist spiritual principles of harmonizing opposites and embracing contradictions.

I'm leaving you with very minimal instruction so you can grasp exactly how simple it is: two symmetrical, interlocking wiggles. Pay close attention to the weaving pattern of this knot, because although it resembles that of many other knots, it doesn't have the predictable over-under-over-under pattern. Some knots, like the Cloud Knot, have an over-over sequence that doubles back in a later step to lock the cord section down. For this reason, you have to follow the diagram steps carefully rather than assuming a pattern. You'll also need to practice some extra patience; it may take you a few attempts to capture the correct tension. Meditate on the process of knotting as you unlock the simple secret of a delicate, curvaceous knot.

cloud knot

loop A under itself

1

A   B

2 Create a second loop with A, then adjust the shape so the first loop is smaller & the second is larger

3

Weave B through, paying close attention to to when B goes "over" & "under" in a loop through the knot

4

Make a small loop with B, weaving in an under-over-under pattern

5

tighten & shape, checking your "over"s & "under"s

WEAVER'S PLAIT

MOVEMENT, THE DANCE OF LIFE, LEGACY OF FIBER ART AND WEAVING

Also called the Ocean Plait, this beautiful woven knot evokes ocean waves on the sea while mimicking the tradition of weaving. This knot is a great example of how fiber art techniques overlap, as the knotting contains an element of weaving within it. The design strongly resembles Celtic knotwork, which is interesting because many Celtic knots are nonfunctioning, fantastical knots—purely imaginative designs to be executed in ink on paper, in metalwork, or in stone, but often incapable of being recreated with cord without significant alteration. This knot, on the other hand, would make a lovely design not only on paper but also with a single cord. If you are a water spirit or a weaver, this knot is for you. Infinite variations of this knot are right at your fingertips; play with building on to it by looping the rope in other spaces or adding in additional cords to weave in and out of the basic design.

Weaver's Plait

fold both cord ends upward in a "U" shape

cross the Right "U" of B over the left "U" of A

Bend B over the top loop & bring it diagonally over the top, tucking the cord end into the bottom right pocket

Weave A diagonally up through the knot

then weave it diagonally back down through the knot

Tighten & shape

PLAFOND

SHELTER/HOME

In French, *plafond* means "ceiling," and this knot was named as such because it resembles the square tiles used for ceilings centuries ago. Its cozy, square design feels like a building block of a home: a tile, a stone block, a tightly clustered neighborhood . . . shelter itself. Make this knot, meditating on feeling its secure, enveloping shape as you think of your dream space. The Plafond is a complicated design that will likely take a few attempts to master, but it is an impressive, compact knot to have in your repertoire.

Several aspects make this knot challenging: matching the lines of your cord to that of the diagram while you work, checking to make sure you follow the correct overs and unders for each step, maintaining the shapes and proportions as you move through the diagram, and tightening. Use a generous number of pins to maintain the correct proportions and check that the negative space and the overs and unders of your knot perfectly match that of the diagram before you continue on to each next step.

Tightening this knot is in fact the most difficult step of them all; you can correctly follow every step and suddenly find your knot falling apart when you begin tightening. To tighten this knot, begin by tightening the center interlocking square shape and gently move the slack down each cord and out the tail, one at a time. Little by little, tighten outward, maintaining the overall proportions as best you can and continuing to ease the slack out of the knot and down the tail.

plafond
knot

1

form the curving shape following the diagram, paying close attention to proportion

2

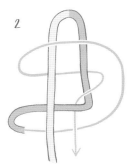

after following the motion, shape up your cord to match the diagram shapes as closely as possible

3

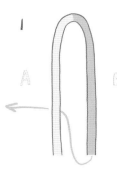

Insert up through the center, looping through & back down

4

weave up through the knot around & back down, paying close attention to maintaining the proportion & looping into the correct places

5

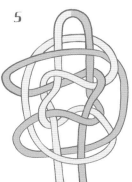

maintaining the loose proportions, begin to slowly

tighten, starting with the center & moving the slack outward & down the tails

6

tightening around the center, starting with the clover shape, follow the slack around the knot & down the tails. The outer loops will be the last to tighten with the hanging loop remaining extended

PIPA KNOT

TRANSCENDENCE, MUSIC, BEAUTY IN ENERGY

The pipa is a traditional Chinese instrument thought to convey the most heavenly sound known on earth. A gently curved string instrument, the pipa has a pear shape similar to a lute. The instrument's size, 3 feet 5 inches, was thought to represent the three realms of heaven, earth, and human, as well as the five elements of earth, wood, metal, fire, and water; the four strings represent the four seasons.

The Pipa Knot, bearing a close resemblance in shape to the instrument, is comprised of gently winding, stacking coils that are secured beautifully by the top coil. Quite unlike most other knots, the Pipa is decorative and often needs extra sewing reinforcement to maintain its shape if jostled. The winding coils are reminiscent of sound waves echoing or the curves of the ear. As noted earlier, the Pipa is a bit different from the other knots in this book and does not maintain the same shape or flow if tied on a vertical knot chain. Its hanging loop is central to the Pipa Knot's design, and the cords exit the knot from different heights and run out together from the back center with no space in between, making it difficult to follow with another knot. Tying the Pipa Knot from two parallel strands would alter the shape of the knot and the vertical knot chain, which may be an interesting place of play and experimentation for you since it is not a traditional rendition.

Another aspect to note is that although this knot is made in a folded construction style like the other knots in this book, the Pipa Knot uses a disproportionate amount of cording on the B (right) strand. Instead of making the folded cord symmetrical with the same length of cord on both sides of the curve, position it so the length of the left strand is the exact length you want your final knot to be, including the tail, and the right strand is many times longer. How much longer depends on the height of the Pipa Knot in proportion to the diameter of the cord.

Pipa knot

CROSS OVER to form the hanging loop

A Remains stationary during the entire knot

Use B to form a large loop below the hanging loop. Make this large loop the size you want your Pipa to be

wrap around the hanging loop

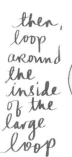

then, loop around the inside of the large loop

making a figure 8

don't stop, keep winding & make a second & third figure 8, looping around the outside of the hanging loop & inside the large loop

Continue making "figure 8's" stacking loops until you fill the large loop frame as completely as possible

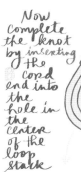

Now complete the knot by inserting the cord end into the hole in the center of the loop stack

gently shape & tighten

Pull down to adjust the hanging loop size

FINISHING AND EMBELLISHING TECHNIQUES

After a knot is tightened to perfection to preserve its shapes, we enter the finishing phase. How much finishing your piece needs is part preference, part design. You can choose to incorporate—or not—any aspect of finishing, including sewing anchor stitches, attaching charms, and adding tassels. If you are just making knots for fun, no finishing is required; but you will need to make a few anchor stitches in strategic places and do some finishing to the cord ends to make sure projects look complete and stay intact when being touched, transported, or jostled. Adding decorative embellishments to your piece can add color, shape, texture, and focus. When you are making jewelry, due to the smaller scale, you'll need a keen eye and steady hand to sew everything to precision. Feel free to use any decorative element to hide the mechanics of construction. Finding a way that doesn't look unnecessarily busy or cluttered is design mastery and can present a lot of fun trial and error toward developing your style.

Anchor Stitches

Sewing is the first step of the finishing phase. As you will see when you work on a vertical knot chain, no knot is an island, so to speak. Each knot, though appearing to be a separate entity, is created on the same strand of cord and is interconnected with all the other knots on the strand. It is easy to zoom in while you are working and forget this connection. You're focusing on perfecting one part of your piece; meanwhile, you've just shifted all the gaps or twists in your rope to other areas. Any twist, gap, slack, or otherwise unwanted flaw in your chain of knots has to be moved down the piece to exit out of the tail to be fully resolved. So, if you were to sew the top of your piece before finishing the bottom, any unforeseen issue where you would need to move an error down the piece would be trapped in the sewn section. The only recourse at that point is to go back and rip out all those stitches. In addition, sometimes you realize that major changes have to happen as you start to approach the end of your piece. For example, you may be running out of cord and want to tighten the top knots to borrow more length for the bottom. For these reasons, it's always best to finish the knotting to completion before adding anchor stitches or embellishments.

Where you make these anchor stitches completely depends on the design of your piece. The objectives with sewing are to reinforce the weakest sections of the knot and keep multiple strands stacked. Wearable pieces contend with more movement and tension than home decor, so they require the most firm and precise stitches at strategic spots to maintain their shape over time. Sections in your piece that include a lot of negative space or weight (especially areas where you plan to add heavy embellishments) will need the reinforcement of a few stitches through nearby cord intersections. Pieces with multiple stacked strands will need stitches through the cords to keep them from flopping, shifting, or collapsing. Tight, compact knots and pieces with lots of interlocking sections often need little to no sewing at all. Wall hangings need to be sewn in a few common spots: on the top of the hanging loop to keep the strands stacked neatly over the hook or nail on which they are hung, at the entry points of the first knot in a vertical knot chain and at the entry point of each subsequent knot, at the cord intersection near any very large loops, and across multiple strands of the tail to keep them lying flat. If you're unsure where to place the anchor stitches, simply pick up your piece by its hanging loop and watch where the cords sink or shift. Those are the points you'll want to stitch.

To anchor a knot, thread a needle with a generous piece of thread that matches the color of the rope or cord you are using and knot the end just as you do when you sew. (If you've never sewn by hand before, pull up a general sewing tutorial on YouTube and practice a few stitches on a scrap piece of cord or fabric.) Find a spot where cords overlap, insert your needle into the back, and pull it through to the front, burying the knot of the thread in the rope or toward the back of the piece. Sew another stitch or two at the place where the cords intersect or any place where the knot needs extra support to hold its shape. After sewing the anchor stitches, either you can pull your needle to the back of your piece again, knot the thread, and trim the excess or you can secure the thread ends inside the cord by making some extra stitches inside one of the cords and trimming the thread, leaving the stitches hidden. If you are unsure where to anchor your knot, simply pick up your work and suspend it to see where it might droop or lose shape if it is hanging on a wall or around a neck.

Sewing through cord or rope is done just like hand sewing through fabric. Double the thread through the eye of a needle and knot the end, making the knot slightly fatter than the needle so it won't slip through as you pull out the needle but still will sink into your cord and be at least partially hidden. Bury the thread knot in an inconspicuous place, such as sandwiched in a cord intersection, so the knot will be tucked away when you pull out the needle.

To make your first anchor stitch, make three or four stitches through the cords to bind them together. Make sure the stitches go *through* the cords so the

stitches are hidden within the cords, rather than over the outside of the cords. Once you have sewn the cords together, complete the anchor stitching by angling your needle toward an inconspicuous place, such as the back of your wall hanging or between cords, so the exit thread will be in another inconspicuous spot. When you pull the needle out of the cord, you can secure the thread in one of two ways. The first option is to sew three or four more stitches hidden within the individual cord your needle came out of. When you pull the thread through completely, repeat the stitch by inserting the needle back through the cord as close as possible to its exit spot. Make a few more stitches inside the interior of the cord. Once it feels sturdy and secure, snip the thread where it exits the cord. Because you added several stitches within one cord, the anchor stitch should be firmly intact. The second option is to finish the anchor stitch, cut the needle off the thread, and make a knot in the spot closest to where the thread exits the rope. Ensure the knot is thick enough that it doesn't slip back through the cord when you pull the cords a bit.

Adding Beads and Charms

Now that you understand how to sew anchor stitches, you can apply the same basic technique to adding beads, stones, and other decorative elements to your piece. Metallic shine beautifully complements the soft, matte quality of fiber cords and tassels. Glass beads and gemstones add an extra dimension of color and shape. Just as you would hand sew a button on a piece of fabric, you can attach any charm with holes to your piece. Round beads can be sewn between cords, tucked into the negative spaces within the knot, charms can be sewn to lie flat on the cord, metal pieces can be added like dangles to the bottom of your knots, and a host of other options are available to you.

Tubes are another popular element to add to knotted cords. Macramé tube beads are commonly wood or metal pipe segments that you can slide onto your cord rather than sewing. To add tubes and similar embellishments to various places within your knotted creations, you will have to slide them on while you work, so it may be best to make a prototype to get a better mental picture of where in the process you will need to slide on the tubes to get the effect you want (see how to make a prototype on page 19). The only requirement is to make sure the hole in the tube is large enough to accommodate your cord. Note that tube diameters are often calculated for the outside diameter of the tube, not the inside

Copper tubes

Brass tubes

Seed beads

Chunky yarn for tassels

thread for sewing

Statement pendants in stone, resin, crystal & brass

Ribbon

Agate Slabs

Chain, jump rings & clasps

drilled crystals

Beads in stone, glass, crystal & resin

Rat tail, fine cord & twine

hole, so be prepared to subtract a millimeter or two to find the inner dimension. Brass charms tarnish over time, so be aware you will need to love the tarnished effect or be prepared to polish your piece occasionally with a brass polishing cloth or liquid polish and cotton swabs. If you are using liquid brass to polish an embellishment, use a very conservative amount and use lots of elbow grease to rub off the tarnish.

To attach an embellishment to your knot, begin just as if you were making an anchor stitch at a cord intersection. Insert the needle in an inconspicuous area where you can bury the knot and exit the needle in the area where you want to sew your charm. Insert the needle through the attachment hole in the charm and back through the cord to attach it. If you are sewing an item into a negative space within a knot, you may be threading the needle through the attachment hole then straight across and through the cord on the other side of the negative space.

After you have made the stitch and the charm is securely in place, make a few invisible anchor stitches to hide the final knot and secure the charm (see page 61).

Pay special attention to the position of a charm's hole when purchasing embellishments. Center-drilled and top-drilled pendants will be suspended differently in your work. If your add-on item is center drilled (the typical hole positioning for beads), it means your stitch will go from the rope, through the entire length of the bead, and into rope on the other side. If your add-on is top drilled, it will be suspended like a pendant from a stitch loop at the top. Look to the spatial proportions on your piece to find the right place for each charm—in fact you may want to design your piece around the charms, allowing the knots to become accents for metal findings. I often allow large empty spaces between knots to frame special gemstones, beads, or tassels.

There are so many beading techniques you might want to explore. As you play and experiment, make sure your charms aren't too heavy for the knot you are sewing it to. If the knot droops or loses shape, the charm is too heavy. This effect can often be remedied by attaching the charm to a more tightly rendered knot, using larger or stronger cord, or doing more anchor stitching at strategic places around the knot to support the charm's weight.

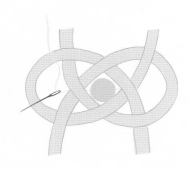

Tassel Making

Go crazy with tassels to add bulk and color to your knot. You can stack and layer tassels together and then sew through their centers so they all are bound on one string. You can even create an ombré effect by stacking tassels of different color gradations on top of one another. Aside from being a similarly decorative element that adds color and texture to your piece, tassels are also a functional way to hide cord ends in a decorative way.

Sewing tassels onto your wall hanging uses exactly the same process as sewing beads or other decorative elements. Pass the thread under the top yarn strand on the top of your tassel; that will serve as a handle for attaching it to your piece. Sew tassels on the outside of knots as a framing element, sew them in the center of negative spaces or within the knot to add bulk and depth, or sew them at the bottom of a knot to hide the exiting cord ends.

Tassels come in three basic variations: a free tassel, a traditional tassel, or a fray.

Free Tassel: The style I call the free tassel is the simplest form, and the one I use most frequently in my work. It is loose and wild and can resemble a colorful hairy creature. It lends itself well to stacking, and because the shape is basic, it doesn't distract from other forms that are intended to draw the eye to the piece. The cons of this type of tassel are that it is difficult to secure it tightly and it has a tendency to shed pieces if it is used on jewelry or another application that has a lot of motion.

Traditional Tassel: The traditional tassel is most likely the kind of tassel you see in your mind's eye: a substantial bundle of somewhat long yarn or cord with a neat, tightly wrapped band at the top. It is a more secure design (pro) that takes a bit more work to complete (con).

Fray Tassel: The fray is the simplest and most natural way to finish a cord ending; it is created simply by fraying a rope end. However, it has a far more limited application because a fray can't be added to other places in the cord without cutting and weakening the cord structure. Another drawback to a fray is that not every cording frays in an aesthetically pleasing way. A fray may be a technique you save for particular cording.

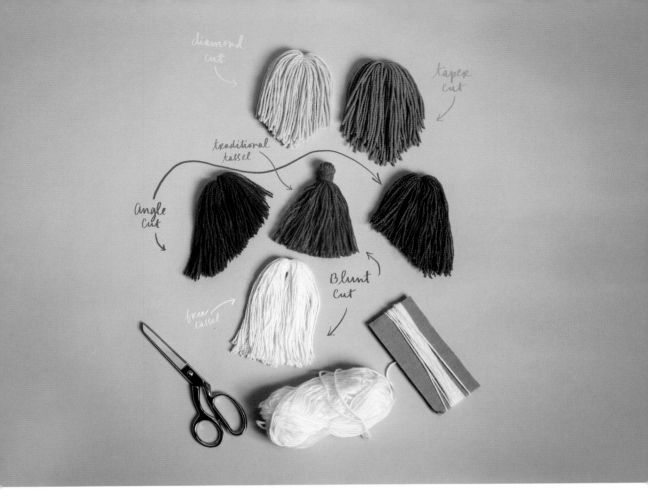

diamond cut

taper cut

traditional tassel

angle cut

Blunt cut

free tassel

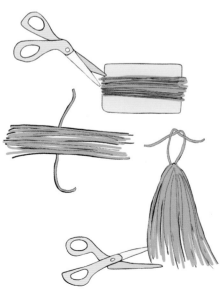

HOW TO MAKE A TASSEL

You'll need a rectangular piece of cardboard, scissors, and a skein of yarn. The rectangular piece of cardboard should measure just slightly longer than the length of the tassel and wide enough so your yarn bundle won't slip off. Note that the width of the cardboard is more about keeping your yarn bundle in place as you wrap the length rather than determining the actual width of the tassel.

1   Cut a 6- to 12-inch-long single piece of yarn. Lay it out straight on the surface area of your workspace.

2   Hold the loose end of the remaining yarn skein and begin to wrap it lengthwise around the cardboard, counting the number of rotations around the cardboard until you have enough yarn to form the ideal fullness for your tassel.

3   When the cardboard is filled, set it flat on the table. Using the scissors, cut across the width of the tassel on one side of the cardboard. Now you have a bundle of many yarn strands falling loose as the cardboard lies on top. Remove the cardboard piece to reveal the cut yarn.

4   Firmly but gently, hold the yarn bundle by one end, keeping the yarn strands even at its blunt cut edge. Lay the bundle of yarn perpendicular across the single piece of yarn you laid on the table.

5   Line the bundle of yarn up so the center of the bundle is lying across the center of the single yarn strand. The shape should resemble a cross. With equal halves of the single yarn strand on each side of your bundle, take one end of the yarn strand in each hand and tie an overhand knot across the bundle as tight and as close to the bundle as possible. Pick up the bundle with one end of the single yarn strand in each hand and pull tightly to use gravity and the weight of the bundle to achieve a tighter knot.

6   Now, seal the knot by tying another overhand knot, double knotting the thread. To get the knot as tight as possible, ask a friend to place a finger on the knot or suspend the bundle so its weight will keep the first knot from loosening while you tie a second knot; tighten well.

7   Time for a haircut! Suspend the tassel from one hand or tack it to a board or wall, then trim the tassel with scissors and cut off any loose hanging threads to make a blunt cut or a layered shag.

Variation: Traditional Tassel

If you wish to make your tassel into a traditional tassel, continue on with this additional step to add a wrapped section near the top of the tassel. You'll need a single strand of yarn 10 to 20 inches long and a tapestry needle with an eye large enough to accommodate the yarn. You can accomplish this step by hand, but a tapestry needle may make it easier to manipulate fine yarns.

1   Lay the free tassel flat in front of you on your work surface.

2   Holding the single yarn strand, create a large loop on one end of the yarn. Lay it on top of the tassel with the dip of the loop facing the bottom of the tassel and the ends positioned toward the top of the tassel: one long end will extend out; one short end will lie near the head.

3   Thread the long end of the yarn strand through the tapestry needle and begin to circle the threaded needle around the circumference of the tassel. Wrap the section near the top of your tassel up to 10 times, spiraling toward the loop in the single strand. Make sure you are wrapping between the loop and the short end of the yarn. The loop and the short end need to be visible when you are done wrapping.

4   When you are finished wrapping, don't unthread the needle. Your tassel in progress will have a little head (the top) and a little turtleneck (wrapping) binding the yarn strands snugly underneath, and you should be able to see both the loop and the short end of the wrapping yarn.

5   Insert the needle into the loop so the threaded yarn is now going through the loop. Unthread the needle.

6   Hold the short end of the loop that is peeking out of the top of the wrapping and gently pull it, shrinking the loop till it disappears under the wrapping.

7   Trim any remaining yarn threads.

Variation: Frayed Cord

Fraying cord ends is by contrast the simplest tasseling method. It's not a way of making an actual tassel, but it offers a similar visional and logistic solution for finishing your cord ends at the tail of your wall hangings. Fraying is untwisting or unbraiding the fibers of your cord to create a voluminous tassel-like effect. This method only works on cords that are made of twisted or braided fibers; it will not work on fabric tubes or leather cords.

1   Put your fingertip flat against the cord and begin to circulate it, gently massaging the cord.

2   Apply more pressure and continue massaging as the cord starts to unwind. (You can also use your hands to physically unbraid or unravel the cord.)

3   Fluff out the fray and check its length as you go, stopping when you have the right proportion.

4   If your yarn has creases coming off of the skein, hold the frayed cord in the air, then dip a wide-tooth comb in water and run it through the tassel. The comb will straighten and order the strands while the water weighs down the kinks and flattens the fiber. Just like hair, cutting when wet with the sharpest possible pair of scissors will bring the cleanest cut.

5   Choose from four different cuts: blunt, angled, diamond, and taper.

- **Blunt:** With the tassel sandwiched between the index finger and middle finger of one hand, run your fingers down to the level you want to cut and use them as a guide to get a straight-across blunt cut. Use your fingers to brace the strands, keeping them taut and in order as you cut.
- **Angled:** Angles can guide the eye up or down to different areas, so an angle cut is great if you want to draw the eye to particular parts of your piece. It doesn't really matter which way you cut the angle, because you can always flip the tassel front or back to use either direction. Similar to cutting the blunt cut tassel, angle your fingers at the inclination and position where you want to cut the tassel and sandwich the strands between them. Use your fingers as a guide to make the cut.
- **Diamond:** This cut is essentially like making an angle cut down both sides so the cuts meet at a center point. The effect is similar to an

upside-down triangle point; however, when you notice the whole tassel is gathered at the top like a point, poufs out toward the sides, and then angles down toward a point at the bottom, it becomes a diamond shape. Estimate the center of the tassel and cut one angle from high on the left down to the center point; then, make a second cut from the right angled down to the center point.

- **Taper:** Think of this cut as giving a fashionable shag haircut to your tassel. Rather than cut across the sides of your tassel as if it were flat, cut into the dimension of the tassel. Hold the tassel in front of you, decide how high up the shortest strands should be cut, position the scissors at that level, and cut into the tassel angling down toward the wall that is opposite you. Your scissors will slice higher on the strands that are closer to you, and lower on the strands that are farther from you. After that initial first angle, gently shake and comb out the tassel and then trim individual strands at levels that are pleasing to the eye. This kind of cut takes longer and is more subjective to the kind of shag look you like best. When finished, the tassel will look wooly and wild in a really beautiful way.

Experimental Embellishments

Throw out the rule book and let your creativity guide the way when experimenting with embellishing your piece! Incorporating elements from other materials and mediums is a great way for both beginning and advanced knotters to express their unique aesthetic. Naturally, beginning knotters often feel more comfortable following traditional knot patterns for the primary structure of the jewelry and wall hangings they create. In this case, a space where they can let their inner voice lead the way would be in choosing embellishments and deciding when and where to sew them. Play with color combinations, texture, and materials to find your aesthetic. More advanced knotters who feel confident in their aesthetic and technique may want to venture out into new challenges like drilling holes into found objects or incorporating other fiber mediums like weaving and needlepoint into their knots.

Use these creative embellishment challenges to exercise your technical skills and imagination. Then create your own!

Make a piece using a knot with ample negative space and sew a charm into each space within the knot. Paying close attention to the design within the negative spaces, choose charms that fill the spaces in an interesting way, and work with the overall composition of the knot.

Create a monochromatic knotted piece—for example, an all-white piece—using four different materials. Experiment with different shades or hues of white and layering textures.

How many tassels could you sew onto a piece? Try to make a piece to support the maximum number of tassels you could possibly imagine. Would you sew them into the negative spaces, around the perimeter of the knot, at each cord intersection, or all of those? Can you layer tassels and play with new color combinations? At what capacity would the tassels begin to obscure the form of the knot?

Do you have craft skills in any other medium that can be incorporated into the piece, such as weaving, wire-wrapping, ceramics, decoupage, dyeing, or woodworking. Try creating pendants in other mediums that can be added into your knotted piece.

PART TWO

KNOTTING PROJECTS

After practicing the knot designs and technical skills, you are now ready to combine the individual techniques you've learned in exciting ways. These projects range in skill level and material pricing, and I offer suggestions for different design routes and lower-cost materials whenever possible. Make sure you have mastered the necessary skills and knots required for the projects that use expensive materials by practicing the techniques with scrap materials (see more on prototyping cords on page 19), and remember to always double-check your measurements before you cut the project cord (it's the only part of knotting that doesn't offer a do-over!).

Read through the project instructions when you gather your materials so you will have an understanding of the trajectory of the project before each step. Allow yourself ample time to dive in and ample space to keep your projects in progress if you don't finish them in one sitting. You may even use these projects as jumping-off points to expand upon and create your own designs. There are endless variations you can make to the projects, even switching out the specific knots for others, while keeping most of the design tenets the same. This section of the book is an educational tool to put your new skills to work and discover the possibilities that knots can offer as adornment, decoration, and functionality.

PIPA KNOT EARRINGS

The Pipa Knot is my personal favorite and a huge inspiration for my own creative work. Since the soft curves echo sound waves and the cup of our outer ears, why not simply place them on ear hooks and turn them into earrings? This project is the simplest application from knot to full-fledged project and demonstrates how even a simple knot can be turned into an adornment with very little additional thought. For a more personal variation, dye your natural cotton cords first with Procion dyes or natural dyes like turmeric. When you are ready to knot, you can work at a table surface or seated at your couch. A knot board or a tray can make you feel more comfortable, though it's not necessary for this knot as it can be tied in your hands and isn't one that requires pins.

Two 29-inch strands Darice 32-ply 3 mm cotton braid macramé cord in natural (Off-White)

Thread in a color that closely matches your cord

Sharp needle

2 earring hooks

1   Use the diagram on page 59 to create identical knots in each strand that measure approximately 2½ inches tall. Tighten and neaten the knots to make them as similar in size and shape as possible. If you are struggling to make them look identical, choose the knot you like best and begin the second one by laying out its pear-shaped frame on top of the Pipa Knot; match the little hanging loop and big curved loop exactly. Complete the knot diagram from there to create two knots of the same size. When you're done, set them aside while you prepare to sew the finishing steps.

2   Cut a 20-inch piece of thread. Double the thread through the eye of a needle and knot the end. Flip the Pipa Knots over so that the back is facing you and begin to sew the ends together. Choose one knot to begin with, and from behind, at the spot just above the bottom of the pipa shape, insert the threaded needle and pull it through the exit cord and out the other side. The knot should now be sandwiched between the exit cord and the back of the Pipa. Complete the stitch by inserting the needle very close to the its exit spot then pulling it through the cord and into the nearest

point on the other exit cord. Just as with normal hand sewing, make sure you are pulling the entire length of thread through as you pull the needle out.

3   Insert the needle into the nearest point on the Pipa Knot and then pull it through the cord and out of the front side of the earring. Insert the needle very close to its exit spot and push the needle through the cord to exit the back of the earring. Complete the square-like stitch pattern to connect the spot the needle exited to the other exit cord. Sew through this other cord, completing a line of stitches that connects the exit cords. Sew one exit cord to the Pipa Knot, and then sew the Pipa Knot back to the second exit cord. Complete your sewing with an anchor stitch by sewing three or four invisible stitches within the exit cord before trimming the thread.

4   Now that the knots are anchored and sturdy, connect them to the earring hooks. Thread the needle in the same way as before. This time, the goal is to bury the thread knot under the arch of the loop by inserting the needle under the arch, sewing upward through the cord, and pulling the needle out of the very top center of your Pipa's hanging loop. Then, insert the needle back near its exit spot at the top of the hanging loop and pull it back through the underside of the loop. Now, make several anchor stitches back through the loop and snip the thread close to the cord. As a final step, cut off the cord tails by slipping one blade of the scissors behind the bottom of the Pipa Knots and the other blade under the tails. Snip with the scissors angled upward so the cord tails will be as inconspicuous as possible when you look at the earrings from the side and front.

MÃE D'ÁGUA NECKLACE AND EARRINGS SET

This earring and necklace set (pronounced MY dee AH-gwah, Portuguese for "Mother of Water") was designed with the Sailor's Breastplate and inspired by the Orisha Yemoja (or *Yemaya* in Spanish and *Iemajá* in Portuguese). She represents motherhood and is a protector of people at sea, often portrayed as a mermaid. Her spirit is present across the African diaspora in various rituals and representations with different name variations. The necklace and earrings are composed of identical knots with long cord ends that are loosely frayed. Each small pendant is like a little amulet of protection. The delicate, organic shape of the pendant is reminiscent of jellyfish or beautiful water plants that drift ashore.

This project will give you an example of how small knots can serve as pendants to adorn the body or objects. Delicate in appearance, yet composed of simple matte cotton rope, the construction is easy and quick, even for a beginner. The necklace requires three knots and the earrings require two, so take note of how many knots you will create if you want to make the earrings and the necklace. Variations can be created by following this simple template with any other knot (or multiple knot designs) in this book and by experimenting with different types of cord and color variations. This project doesn't require a knotting board or pins to complete.

1 spool 4 mm single strand cotton rope in lilac (or color of your choice)

Thread

Sharp needle

2 earring hooks

1. For each pendant, cut two 23-inch strands of cord. To make your first pendant, lay the two strands of cord in front of you in a bell curve shape with the center of the strands at the top of the peak. Following the diagram on page 51, knot the two cords into the Sailor's Breastplate simultaneously. Gently tighten the knot until there is no negative space and the knot takes on a star shape that is approximately 1½ inches wide with five soft peaks around the perimeter and two long exit cords that measure at least 3½ inches. Repeat for the remaining pendants.

2   Once the knots are finished, take the end of the thread, and with the remainder still on the spool, begin to wrap it snugly around the tails at the base of the knot (the exit point). Don't be concerned with stacking each thread neatly; any way you wrap it will be fine. Continue wrapping quickly and evenly around the exit point of the knot until it feels secure and the wrap measures approximately 1/8 inch high. When you are ready to end the wrap, cut the thread off the spool at least 6 inches from the knot. Place the thread end through the needle and pass it through the wrapping and the cords and out the other side of the knot. Inserting the needle as close as possible to its exit spot, pass the needle back into the wrapping, through the cords, and out the other side. Snip the excess thread to end the wrapping.

3   Fray the cord ends by gently pulling the strands apart then dividing each cord end into four or more parts. You could also gently run a fine-tooth comb through the cords to divide them. Once the fray is made, measure 3 inches (only the fray below the wrapping) and make a blunt cut across that point with scissors. Repeat these steps for each pendant.

4   To create the necklace, cut a 38-inch piece of cord. Measure the midpoint where you will attach the center pendant. Thread the needle with a 12-inch piece of thread and pass it through the center point of the cord strand twice to create two stitches inside the cord. Now position the needle approximately 1/8 inch down from the top of the pendant, insert it, and pull it through the other side. Bring the needle back over and around the cord midpoint, insert the needle at the same spot 1/8 inch from the top of the pendant, and stitch through the back of the pendant. Continue this wrapping motion several times but pass the needle through different spots at the top of the pendant until the wrap is approximately 1/8 inch wide. Your goal is to mimic the thread wrap thickness and size you made at the base of the pendant. To attach the other two

pendants, measure 2½ inches from both sides of the cord's midpoint and follow the same instructions for attaching them to the cord.

5   With the pendants on the cord, place the necklace against yourself to see where it lies best. A common length is 30 inches, with the cord measuring 15 inches from each side of the center pendant to the back of your neck. It can be secured with a double-knotted overhand knot (the knot for tying your shoes). This knot can be tied and untied to take the necklace on and off, but it is best tied once and then slipped on and off over the head to preserve the cord. Once you find your necklace length, mark the spot on each strand with a small piece of tape or a pin. On each side, measure 2 inches from the piece of tape toward the cord end and snip the excess.

6   To make the earrings, cut a 10-inch piece of thread, place it through the needle, and knot the ends together. Hold the knot vertically in the air and pass the needle vertically down through the center top of the knot and angled out the back approximately ⅛ inch down from the top of the pendant. Double back, passing the needle back through the exit spot in the back and out of the top of the knot. Now, pass the needle through the attachment loop of the earring hook and down through the top of the pendant, directing the needle out the back approximately ⅛ inch from the top. Continue this motion three or four more times, passing through the earring hook loop, down through the top of the pendant, and out the back to create a tiny wrapping that's barely visible at the back of the earring. Your attachment wrapping needs to be fairly tight so the hook seamlessly attaches to the pendant and is flush to the knot without any gap. To end your hook attachment, pass the needle down through the knot and out the back approximately ½ inch from the top; cut the thread.

KNOT SEQUENCE: MANIFESTING DREAMS

This project has been a staple of my creative practice and the primary project that I teach to help beginners understand knotting. Through this project, you will touch upon all the basic techniques necessary to knot decorative works and connect the symbolic significance of knots to your personal life. In this project, you will create a vertical knot chain wall hanging using basic knots that represent your personal dreams, intentions, or goals. Creating this piece will allow you to dive deep into the personal connection and mindfulness of knotting. You'll learn not only knotting, tassel making, and sewing construction, but also how to flex your creative muscles by making key design choices.

In the instructions below, I'll walk you through designing your own piece. If you'd rather create the specific design that's pictured, refer to the photo (page 86) for the information on length required, strands, knot design, and tassel placement; you'll find the specs that walk you through creating the Cross-Cloud Wall Hanging after the instructions.

This project can be endlessly varied to include any folded construction, but you may want to use a different knot, make more knots in your chain, add tassels to various spots, or sew or string beads and charms on your piece.

50 feet ³/₈-inch cotton braid rope

1–4 skeins yarn of your choice, for tassels

Darning needle

Thread in color that matches your rope

Knot board and pins

One 10 x 7-inch or larger piece cardboard

Optional: Charms, beads, tubes, or drilled stones

1 Journal or doodle to define some dreams or intentions for your life and home and select from two to four different knots to reflect these ideas in your design. You can make your design with two or four strands of rope. Two-strand designs tend to be longer and have an elegant look, whereas four-strand designs tend to be shorter and fuller. If your design has four knots or even two ornate knots, it will require more length, so plan to make your wall hanging two strands and see pages 17–19 on estimating rope length. As you prototype your project, keep in mind that each outer strand will be making a wider pathway and will require more rope than the innermost strand. Spacing between knots and creating space to sew amulets will also need to factor into your design and overall rope length.

Look through the Basic Knots section (pages 39-59) to explore what knots you connect with on a personal level. Any knot with two entry points and two exits points that can be created with the folded construction method will suffice (page 35). Here is a list of other knots and their meanings, aside from those in this book, that you may want to consider for this project:

Double Connection – Communication

Good Luck – Luck

The Wing Knot – Travel

Ring of Coins – Completion

Box Knot – Security

Trinity Knot – Spiritual Trinity

2   Given the amount of rope required for this project, I suggest working on the floor or standing at a table with a couple feet of room in each direction to work. With your knots selected, prepare your rope. Undo the 50-foot hank of rope and find the center by laying it out and folding it in half; add a piece of tape around the circumference to mark the center. Cut two 25-foot strands of rope from the center of this taped section. If you are making a four-strand piece, hold the two strands together, then fold them in half again, marking the center and cutting the ends to create four separate strands.

3   Pin each strand at the center to the top of your knot board, stacked one on top of the other. Starting from the center of the rope, make the first knot, referring to the diagram. Once the knot is complete, shape the hanging loop to the size you want and tighten and smooth out any kinks in the knot. Work one side at a time and always start at the top, easing the kinks and slack out at the tail.

4   Continue to make each knot in the sequence with the exit point of the last knot becoming the entry point of the next knot. After each knot is complete, work from top to bottom and trace your hands across the pathways of Side A then Side B. Your goal is to find and ease any twists, gaps, or excess slack out at the exit points and down the tail. Make sure your strands are evenly stacked and look toward the negative space within the knot designs to double-check that the proportions are balanced. How much space you leave between knots is a personal preference: you can leave a large window to allow a charm or tassel to be sewn within it and framed by the rope, or you can stack each knot flush on top of one another without any spacing in between.

5   When you have finished knotting and smoothing out the knot sequence, sew the anchor points following the photo on the next page and the instructions on

page 61. Make your tassels following the instructions on page 67. Determine the length of the tassels by holding a cardboard piece or a measuring tape up to the spots where you want to place them. Gauge exactly how long you want them to be and add ¼ inch. Cut one side of the cardboard piece to that specific length. Wrap the yarn around the cardboard until you get the thickness you like—anywhere from 40 to 100 wraps, depending on how thick the yarn is. Attach the tassels to the knot anywhere along the bottom or sides, from loops, or within windows of space. Hang your piece on the wall and comb the tassels after they are attached. Add a bit of water to the comb or use a spray bottle to dampen the tassels as you comb. Give the tassels a final trim while they are damp and straight.

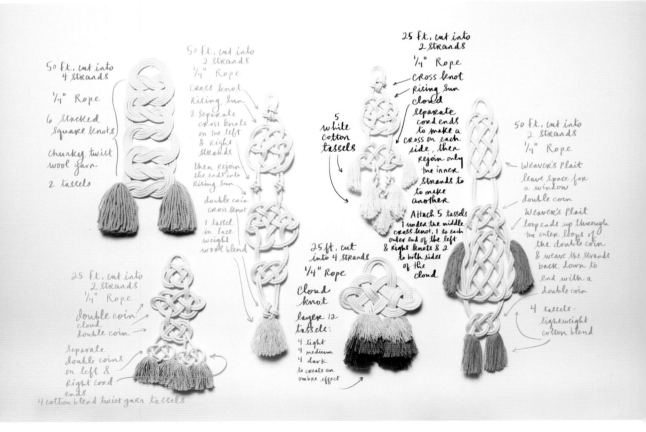

6   If your piece ends in a knot, tape off the tails about 1½ to 3 inches below the exit point, cut the rope, and then remove the leftover tape. If your design ends with tassels, tape off a spot on your cords about 1½ inches from the place where the tassel is sewn, then cut and remove the remaining tape. Your design is best hung on a wall by resting the hanging loop on a clear pushpin. You can hang your piece on nails, but I find that clear plastic pushpins have the chunkiness to support the rope, whereas nails are usually too slim.

Cross-Cloud Knot

Rope prep:
50 feet of rope cut into
4 strands of 12½ feet

Design sequence:
Cross Knot (page 46)

Cloud Knot (page 52)

TASSELS

1   Choose three colors in the same tone—one light, one medium, and one dark—to create an ombré effect. Make four freestyle tassels measuring 6 inches long in each color. At the very bottom of the finished knot, sew two light tassels to the left-side cord tails: one sewn to the outer tail and the other sewn to the second tail strand from the inside. Do the same to attach the two remaining light tassels to the right-side cord tails, making sure they are sewn level across the tails. Now, at the halfway point, approximately 3 inches from the top and bottom of the light tassels, make a similar row of medium tassels sewn to the same tails underneath the light tassels. Last, find the halfway point of the medium tassels and sew the dark tassels in a row across the same tails. You now have an ombré effect tassel section at the bottom of your Cloud Knot. Finish the cord ends, and comb the tassels accordingly.

SATIN BOOKMARK

This project is a smaller version of the Knot Sequence project (page 83). A thinner, silkier cord is an excellent challenge to hone your skills. Be sure to work with lots of pins, plenty of lighting, and your knot board. You can choose a silk or budget-friendly nylon satin rattail, but if you are struggling with slippery cords, try a sturdy, hollow cotton macramé. The key to a successful bookmark is the cord flatness, which allows the finished project to lie nicely when the book is closed. For that reason, it's best to use mat knots in a cord that flattens with weight (this design includes a three-dimensional Cross Knot at the top to peek out of the book). Another important way to make the bookmark lie flat is to alternate which cord is "in" and which cord is "out" on the left and right entry points of each knot. Knot sequences have a tendency to twist in a particular direction if all the knots in the sequence have the out cords on the same entry point side, so I've included diagrams for the reverse version of the Weaver's Plait to use for the third and fifth knots. If you would like to make a bookmark without tassels to cover the ends, burn the ends of the nylon rattail with a lighter or match to seal the cord. (Note: this will not work for silk rattail, because natural fibers do not melt like synthetics.)

172 inches satin finish silk or nylon rattail in color of your choice (I used silk cord in violet)

Knot board and pins

Silk embroidery thread in color of your choice (I used plum)

One 4–7 mm x 6–12 mm bead of your choice (I used a teardrop moonstone)

Thread in a color that matches your cord

materials list continues on page 90

1   Fold the rattail cord in half once and then in half again. Lay out the cord in a double-strand, folded construction style on your knot board and snip the doubled cord end, resulting in a two-strand bell curve. Determine the hanging loop size, then work through each of the knots in this order: Cross Knot (page 46), Weaver's Plait (page 54), Reverse Weaver's Plait (pictured in the diagram), Double Coin (page 44), and ending with Reverse Weaver's Plait again. As you work, smooth and order the cord to match the diagram's proportions and spacing.

2   Sew anchor points with a sharp needle, as marked on the diagram (you can add more as needed). Add 12 to 24 inches of thread to your needle, doubled and knotted at the end. If you have magnifying glasses, they will come in handy to avoid pulling the fibers, creating creases, or making loose stitches while beading and sewing. As you sew, gently pull the needle through the

Beading needle

Sharp needle

4 x 3-inch piece cardboard

Optional: Jeweler's magnifying glasses or magnifying lamp

cord and sandwich the knotted end of thread between cords to hide them. Last, use a beading needle to sew on the bead, suspending it from the top center intersection of the Double Coin as shown in the diagram (see pages 63–65 for instructions on sewing beads onto your piece).

3   Create five traditional-style tassels following the instructions on page 70 and cut them to approximately 2½ inches long, referring to the diagram for placement. Sew through the cord to bury the knot, then pass the threaded needle under the loop of the tassel head and back through the cord to attach it. Create anchor stitches through both cords after attaching the tassels for reinforcement. To attach the top tassel, cut a strand of tassel yarn or silk thread, and thread it through a sharp needle. Pass the needle under the loop of the tassel head so the tassel is centered on the strand. Double knot the strand snuggly around the tassel head. Then, fold the thread tails around the hanging loop so the tassel head is about 1½ inches away, and double knot it around the hanging loop. Trim the excess thread.

4   To finish, follow this step on both sides of the bookmark: Insert a threaded needle into the cord tails approximately 1 inch below the exit points and circle the needle around the cords to tightly wrap them seven or so times. Insert the needle back through the wrapping and make three anchor stitches; trim the thread. Last, trim the cord ends a few millimeters below the wrapped section.

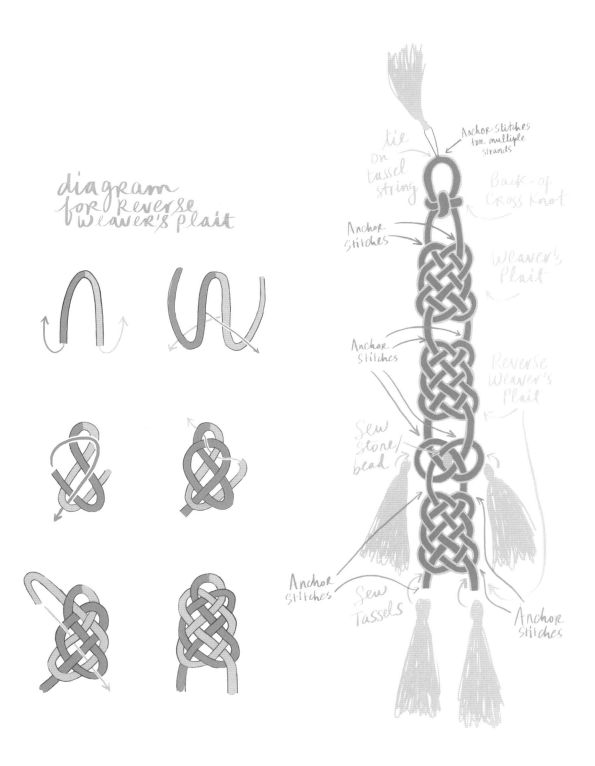

diagram
for Reverse
weaver's plait

tie on tassel string

Anchor stitches for multiple strands

Back of Cross Knot

Anchor Stitches

Weaver's Plait

Anchor Stitches

Reverse Weaver's Plait

Sew stone/ bead

Anchor Stitches

Sew Tassels

Anchor Stitches

SUN WORSHIPPER
STATEMENT NECKLACE

For this wearable statement necklace you will be reworking the Sun Cycle Knot to subtly evoke a large heart. This project is an exercise in both tightening to reimagine traditional knots and the do-it-yourself cord-making skill called wrapping. Necklaces that use macramé style knotting often use symmetrical construction, but because this pendant is an elaborate knot, we will use a folded construction to create the knot (see page 35); then, we'll flip our work upside down to work upward and finish the sides and clasps of the necklace.

The Sun Worshipper Statement Necklace combines knotting and wrapping in the style I have developed for my jewelry line. Before knotting, the cord must be wrapped, and this project lets you get your feet wet with the technique. You'll be wrapping just the pendant portion of the cord in a thick yarn, which introduces you to the technique while cutting down on time and energy. This partially wrapped cord creates a focal point by drawing the eye to the colorful pendant you can wrap in any hue. The 3/8-inch rope makes a great size for a chunky statement necklace. To make a slimmer piece, shift to 1/4-inch rope. For other variations, experiment with pairing yarn wrap colors with different rope colors and textures, for example, a twist rope instead of a braid.

One 90-inch piece 3/8-inch cotton braid rope

Lion Brand 24/7 cotton yarn in goldenrod

50 inches 2 mm silk rattail in gold

Tapestry needle or chenille needle

Permanent marker or 2 small rubber bands

Pins

Crochet thread or embroidery thread in a color that matches the rope

1   The first step in the creation of this piece is wrapping the cord. Measure 21 inches in from one rope end and 17 inches in from the other cord end; wrap a rubber band around each spot or place a dot with the marker to indicate the boundaries of the yarn wrapping. The 21-inch side will be the side with the clasp loop, and the 17-inch side will be the side with the clasp button. Both marker spots will be covered with thread later.

2   To make the rope more manageable as you are wrapping it, choose an end and begin to bundle it up by wrapping the rope around itself or around your hand. Continue wrapping past your first marker until you get 10 to 12 inches from your second marker. Tighten the bundle and insert the rope end into the hole in the

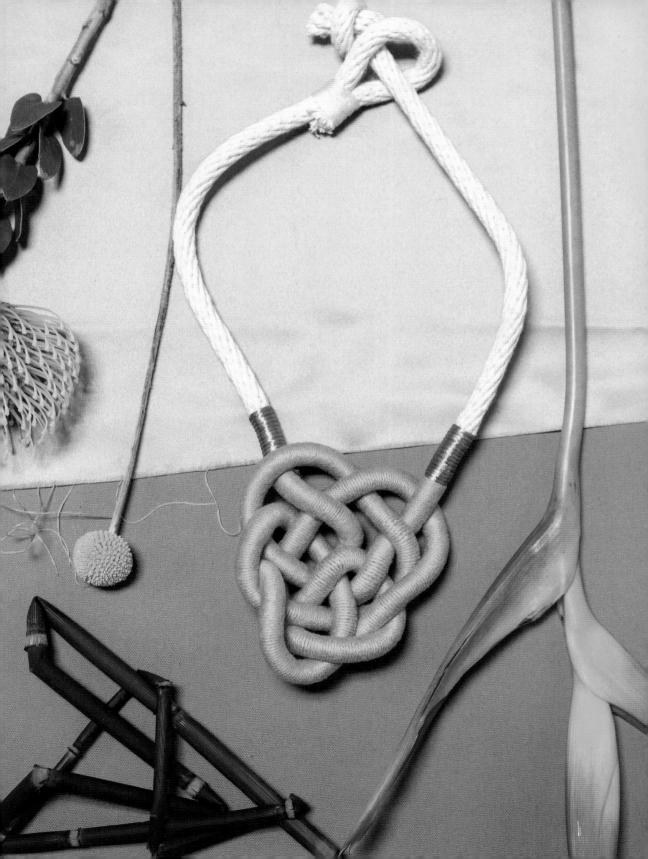

center of the coil to keep the rope securely bound. How exactly you coil or knot this bundle doesn't matter—it may look like a messy tangle or a neat rope bundle. The objective is to bundle it into a compact tangle that is loose enough that you can release rope as you wrap in that direction. Now, tightly coil the other end of the rope until you get to the second marker, leaving 10 to 12 inches of naked rope ready to wrap.

3   In this step you will wrap from one marker to the other, releasing naked rope every so often from your large bundle and bundling up the wrapped rope as you go. First, take the end of the yarn on the skein and tie it around the circumference of the second marker in a simple overhand knot with 1 or 2 inches of yarn hanging from the end. Once the yarn is secure, you can discard or ignore your marker. Now, holding the smaller bundled section of rope in your nondominant hand, begin to swing the rope in a circle using the heavy bundle's momentum, swirling clockwise like a pendulum, while your dominant hand holds the yarn taut to position and steady the wrapping coils. Fairly effortlessly the yarn will orbit the circling rope in a clockwise direction, slowly and snuggly stacking the spiraling yarn around the circumference of the rope. As you wrap, keep an eye on the way the yarn is spiraling around the rope. Stop to shift the yarn and close any gaps that occur or to untwist any overlap or a tangle. You can judge exactly what length of rope is comfortable for you to wrap between the bundles, how often you release more naked rope from the big bundle, and how often you add the newly wrapped rope to the smaller knotted section. Continue moving down the rope until you reach the first marker at the end of the rope. When the rope is wrapped completely between both markers, the last step is to cut the yarn to leave a 4-inch tail and tie the yarn end around the rope in an overhand knot, allowing the yarn tail to dangle.

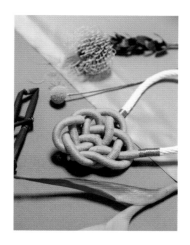

4　Lay the wrapped rope in front of you in the bell curve shape with the center of the wrapped section at its peak. Weave the Sun Cycle Knot following the diagram on page 49. Once it is complete, tighten the knot beyond its normal form. As you shape, mold, and tighten, the knot will begin to look like a heart. It will reach the right degree of tightening when the knot is well contained within the wrapped cord. When the Sun Cycle Knot is tightened sufficiently it will measure a little over 4 inches wide and 5 inches tall, and the wrapped section will continue approximately 2 inches beyond the knot exit points.

5　Now, flip the cord so the top of Sun Cycle Knot is at the bottom and the rope ends are at the top. Your knot is now the pendant at the bottom of the necklace, and the rope ends will be the cords extending upward to hang it from your neck. Eye the point where the exit cord crosses over or under the pendant on either side and aim to end your wrapping exactly there. Untie the yarn ends and unwrap the yarn until you hit the top of the exit points. On one side, that point should be around 19 inches from the end, and on the other side, it should be around 23 inches from the end. Place an overhand knot at each point to secure the spot. Flip the necklace over to take a look at the back side. Your necklace will be nearly identical on both sides, but you may have a side you prefer or a side that lies better on the body. Note that your preferred side is the front.

6　To finish the yarn wrapping, untie one of the overhand knots and thread the tail end of the yarn through a needle. Position the threaded needle at the exit point on the back of your necklace and insert it through the rope. Once you pull the needle through, sew another stitch inside the rope by passing through the rope again and then trim the yarn end. You always do this at the back of your necklace so that the points where the wrapping starts or stops are less conspicuous. Once you have one side of the wrapped cord neatly ended, repeat the process at the other exit point.

7   With the pendant knot complete, add wrapped satin rattail accents on each side of your pendant. Gold satin rattail is the ideal accent because its shiny, smooth, metallic surface draws attention to your soft matte gold knot. Wrap the rattail in the same fashion as you wrapped the yarn, but begin by threading one end of the needle with the rattail, drawing it through the back of the rope and out the other side. Anchor it with a final internal stitch by drawing the needle back through the rope again; trim the rattail end. From this firm anchor point you can begin to wrap the rattail toward the rope end. Because you have such a short rope end to contend with, you do not need to bundle that end; you can let it swirl loosely around your hand or arm as you wrap. Hold the pendant in your nondominant hand, and hold the rattail bundle in the other. Swirl the rattail around the rope using the same wrapping technique you used earlier. Wrap the rattail around the naked rope sides approximately 1½ inches from both exit points of the pendant toward the cord end. You can stop whenever it looks good to your eye. To end the rattail, cut it from the bundle, leaving a 4-inch tail. Thread the chenille or tapestry needle with the rattail end, insert it through the rope, and repeat a final stitch through the rope before cutting off the excess rattail.

8   The final step is to create the clasps, but you first need to know exactly how long to make your necklace. To allow leeway for different necklace lengths and space for the clasp, I planned for the rope ends to be sufficiently longer than you will probably need. I recommend making the necklace length so that

the pendant sits comfortably in the center of the mid-chest. Everyone has a different length from the back of their neck to the center of their chest, so the best way to choose the length is to look in a mirror and hold the necklace against yourself. When you find the right length, mark the spots with pins in the rope (pins standing up; sharp side in the rope but not sticking out the other side) or rubber bands.

9   It's hard to find sufficient hardware for large-diameter cords, so the following clasps can be used in a pinch. The hook-and-eye and the button loop are two of the simplest clasps, and the version used with this necklace relies on the same principle. One side of the rope will serve as the hook (or loop), which latches around a "button" on the other side, which is basically just a wide shape that gets caught in the loop. The button for this necklace will be a chunky overhand knot on the shorter cord side that is positioned just above the spot you marked at the center of your neck. Make a simple overhand knot just above the pin and tighten the knot by pulling both ends of the cord as hard as possible. Trim the excess cord approximately 1 inch above the knot. To finish the cord end, you can either add jewelry glue to the end and let it sit overnight so the cord won't fray or manually fray the cord for an organic look. If your knot is sturdy enough, you can simply trim the end closer to the knot.

10 For the hook end on the other cord, fold the rope into a loop. Tighten the loop so the button just barely fits when you push it through. You don't want your loop so big that your button easily slips out, nor so small that your button won't fit through the loop at all. Test the loop by fitting it over the button until you find the right fit; then, place a pin or two through the base of the loop where you will close it off. Now, use the wrapping

technique once again to seal the loop. Thread the needle with a 12-inch piece of embroidery thread, doubled at the needle, and knot the ends. Draw the needle through the center of the loop base, between the ropes, and pull it out the other side. Make sure the thread knot is resting right at the pinch of the base where you first inserted your needle. Double back and insert your needle through a place in either rope at the loop base near the needle's exit spot. Stitch between the two ropes two or three times at the top of the loop base; stitch through the rope so your work is not visible on the surface. The thread knot should be securely hidden somewhere between the ropes at the loop base, and the loop should feel secure. Test the loop by fitting it over the button to ensure a snug fit. Ideally, the loop should fit over the button with a little push from your hand, similar to the effort of fitting a tight T-shirt neck hole over your head. Then, begin to wrap approximately ½ inch down from the top of the loop base spiraling the threaded needle around and around the loop base, stacking each row of wrapping below the previous one, working down in the direction of the pendant. Because you are dealing with such a fine thread, the wrapping doesn't have to be perfect, just try to get a fairly clean wrapped stack as you spiral down the rope. When you have covered approximately ½ inch, insert your threaded needle into the rope that is opposite the rope end and draw it out. Make four to six stitches around the spot where you inserted the needle. Do not pass through the other rope because most of that rope will be cut. Once you're finished, snip the thread. Try on your necklace as a triple-check to see how it looks. If it is too loose or too tight you will have to cut the embroidery thread and redo this wrapping step at a higher or lower point until you get the right fit. When you are happy with the fit, snip the cord end under the loop's wrapping. You may opt to dab jewelry glue on this cord end to further secure it.

CROSS KNOT
STACKING BRACELET

This bracelet makes a quick and simple project that is great for beginners and suitable even for older children. The bracelet is composed of an X shape that folds around the wrist in an unconventional construction—the hanging loop for the Cross Knot becomes the space for your wrist to fit into. This project inspires you to reimagine the dimensions of traditional knots. For a project variation, stack multiple bracelets on your arm in the same color, alternating colors, or in a rainbow of colors. Testing different bead and cord color pairings will stretch your imagination even further.

One 24-inch piece 2 mm waxed cotton cord in color of your choice

1 seed bead in color of your choice

Beading needle

Thread in a color that matches your cord

1 set magnetic connector clasps with a 2–3 mm hole (I used a 12 mm-long clasp)

1   Before beginning, decide where you want your bracelet—or bracelets if you are making more than one—to rest on your arm. Keep in mind that even though there is a clasp, you will need to slip the bracelet over your hand to put it on, so the smallest bracelet will probably fall an inch or more below your wrist. Envisioning how you want the bracelets to fall will determine which part of your arm to measure when you are creating them. If you are making a large group of bracelets to stack (six or more), be mindful that you will need to measure each part of your arm where they will fall in order to get them to stack nicely.

2   Take the piece of waxed cotton cord, center the midpoint of the cord on your arm, and measure where the bracelet will fit comfortably around your wrist with a little space and use pins to mark the spot. Lay the pinned cord on the table. The large gap from the center point of the cord to the spot with the pins is the hanging loop, which will be transformed into the wrist loop. Waxed cotton cord has a stretch that should allow the loop to fit over your fist. The place where both spots meet is where you should position your Cross Knot.

3   Holding the intersection of the cording in your hand, remove the pins and weave the Cross Knot in that spot following the diagram on page 47. Once you have created the knot, check the size by slipping the open circle over your hand to ensure it fits over the widest part of your hand. If it doesn't fit, tighten or bring more slack into the knot to adjust the size.

4   When the knot is correctly positioned, sew the bead into place in the center of the Cross Knot. Cut a 16-inch piece of thread identical to the cord color, thread it through the needle, and knot the ends. Insert the needle through the cords at the bottom center of the knot and pull the thread through until the thread knot is buried in the center bottom of the knot. Bring the needle back up through the knot by inserting it as close as possible to the needle's exit spot. Pull the threaded needle up through the center of the Cross Knot and string a seed bead on the needle so it falls down the thread into the center of the knot. Now, insert the needle back into any cord inside the Cross Knot to create the loop that secures the bead in the center of the knot. Tighten the exiting cords of the knot around the bead and make sure it is secure. Then, create some invisible stitches by sewing in and out through the waxed cord three to five times to make anchor stitches; snip off the remaining thread.

5   Now that the bead is attached, the final step is to create the clasp. Although the loop of the bracelet must slip over the hand to put it on, a second set of exit cords are given clasps to create the X shape of the bracelet as it wraps around the wrist. Match the exit cords to the size of the wrist loop, stringing the clasp hardware on each side, doubling the cord over, and placing a pin through the cord loop to mark the spot where the clasp needs to be attached. To begin sewing one clasp loop in place, thread a needle with 24 inches of thread doubled on the needle—no need to knot the

end. Insert the needle through the cords and out the other side to secure the clasp piece in the loop. Pull the needle out until you get to the last 2 inches of thread. Create a second and third stitch by inserting the needle back through the cords and out the other side. Now, begin to wrap the threaded needle around the base of the loop ten to fifteen times and insert the needle back through the cords to end the wrap. Sew through the cords to create a couple more stitches. Clip the thread and the original 2-inch tail. Repeat these steps to secure the other side of the clasp to the other cord.

COLORBLOCK WOVEN
KNOT PANEL

The soft, plush, wool-felted cords and natural fiber yarns color-blocked in rich warm tones create a delicious combination. This project is certainly the most ambitious one in this book due to its intricate design and premium materials. Enjoy diving into the soft textures and inviting hues as you work, taking note of how the colors play against one another and how different pairings elicit different moods. Consider how you can experiment with color and texture combinations in your own practice. Perhaps you can even scale this project up or down to create an impressive colorblock panel in other hues. This design can also be used for surface applications. Doubling or quadrupling the panel and omitting the side tassels would create an impressive indoor accent rug or plush surface for a table. The felted cords suggested in this tutorial are best suited for application as a wall hanging, so using rope or other sturdy cording would increase the durability of a rug in high-traffic areas. For use as a table cover, a thinner, smoother cord like a hollow, woven cotton cord would offer a flatter, less fuzzy appearance.

The suggested materials to make this piece can be pricey, so I recommend prototyping the interlocked Weaver's Plaits in rope. If the cost of materials is a primary concern, try making the entire piece in only one or two alternating colors to reduce the amount of cord used to less than two 50-yard balls. As you journey through fiber, searching for specific yarns you've used for past projects, you might notice the unfortunate occurrence of fiber companies discontinuing styles and colors every so often. If anything listed here is discontinued or not available in your area or online, all is not lost. I chose each tassel yarn by taking small cord samples to my local yarn shop for color matching; you can do the same. The yarns I used are different weights. They range from medium weight to super bulky because the chunkier sizing leads to a more seamless continuation of the felted wool cord, and larger-weight fibers take less yarn and less work to make the huge tassels required.

Essentially this piece consists of four separate Weaver's Plaits that have been linked by weaving the perimeter cords through the negative space within the adjoining plaits. The first Weaver's Plait is knotted as usual, but the subsequent knots are knotted by pulling the cords through the spaces within the previous knot so that each is a separate knot linked through the knots next to it. To finish the piece, the cord ends are sewn to the back and neatly cut, and the four corner intersections and middle section are sewn together for added support. The tassels are sewn through the cords at eight different points around the perimeter of the piece. Any mat knot can be used as a flat panel wall hanging or table accent, so this basic design can be varied endlessly when you experiment with other cording, colors, and knots.

Four 50-yard balls Love Fest Fibers Tough Love cord in 4 different colors (I used Natural White, Rose Gold, Turmeric, and Terracotta)

6 large skeins yarn in colors corresponding to each cord (I used Mirasol Ushya in White Clouds, Mirasol Ushya in Beehive Yellow, Amano Puna in Inca Ruins, Knit Collage Sister in Dusty Pink Heather, and Quince & Co. Puffin in Dogwood. All are chunky weight yarns except Amano Puna)

One 12 x 12-inch piece cardboard

Thread in a neutral color

1 soft sculpture needle

1   This piece is actually knotted upside down and backward from how it will be displayed. You will begin working counterclockwise from the bottom left in this order: terracotta plait, turmeric plait, rose gold plait, and white plait. Find a comfortable, spacious spot to work, and please note that this piece is best constructed while sitting on the floor with ample space or when standing at a large, empty table.

2   To begin the first terracotta Weaver's Plait, cut four pieces of Tough Love cord that each measure 180 inches long. While you can knot all four strands simultaneously, I recommend knotting a single strand to start and then weaving the other three strands into the knot individually. Weave the Weaver's Plait following the diagram on page 55. Beginning with the first strand of cord, lay out the yarn in a bell curve approximately 22 inches tall. Once you have completed the knot, begin to smooth, unwind, and order the strands while tightening the overall shape. Tighten and proportion the four-strand Weaver's Plait until the knot measures approximately 20 inches tall and 13 inches wide; the set of eight exiting cord strands at the bottom of the knot will measure 16 inches or more. (Note: You may need to make adjustments, so don't cut any of the exiting cords until after each plait is completed and the sewing is finished.)

3   To make the second plait and subsequent plaits, cut four 180-inch-long pieces of Tough Love cord. The

diagram on page 108 shows what loops to link the strands through as you knot them. As you knot, the strands of the turmeric plait will pass through each outer loop on the right side of the terracotta plait. These natural open spots align with the curvature of the turmeric strands when the knots are side by side. After knotting with a single cord, weave in the three other strands of cord, then tighten and shape the turmeric knot to match the exact size, shape, and proportion of the terracotta knot. Allow comfortable spacing so the two knots are beautifully linked and lying flat, not bunched together or tight.

4   Next, begin the rose gold plait in the same manner, linking the strands through the top two loops of the turmeric knot. Note that the rose gold plait does not interlock with the terracotta plait. Finally, create the white plait while passing the strands through the three loops of the left side of the rose gold plait at the same points where the terracotta and turmeric knots link. The white plait will also loop into the top of the terracotta knot.

5   When all the knots are completed and linked up, ensure they are all smooth and the strands lie in order, free of any twists, bunches, or gaps. Now, flip the piece over and turn it upside down so that the terracotta knot is in the top left and the turmeric knot is in the top right. Lift the piece from the top loops of the terracotta and turmeric knots to see how it hangs, eyeing the piece as a whole to check to see if each knot is close to identical in proportion. Although it is not yet anchored (sewn), you should be able to see if there are any large gaps that need to be tightened and where you will need to sew for reinforcement. Once the piece is sufficiently tightened, you can begin sewing it in place. Start by sewing key intersections in the center of the piece where the colors come together. The outer intersections where the turmeric and rose gold strands connect and

where the white and terracotta intersections connect are of primary concern, as well as the center of the piece where all of the loops intersect.

6   Sew the top two corners of your piece. Starting with the terracotta knot, pull the strands of the left exit point out of the corner loop and wrap them around the outside of the loop and around the back. Fold them up and behind the left corner. Now, take the strands at the right exit point and bring them up and around the back, pulling them through the top left loop, over the left exit point strands, and back into the loop. The right exit point strands are now exiting the knot diagonally, extending down. These are the new exit points for the top cords to finish the piece.

7   Sew the left exit cords in place behind the top left loop, sewing across the exit cords and into each cord of the top left loop. Sew the right exit cords to the back of the top left loop in a similar manner. Keep in mind, after all the anchor points are sewn in place, you will be cutting off the cord ends, so the sewing you do now should secure the proportions and allow for the ends to be completely hidden once the excess cord is trimmed.

8   Next, follow a similar, mirror image design for hiding the exit cords on the right corner with the turmeric knot. Wrap the right exit cords back behind the right loop. Now, pull the left exit cords to the right and loop them over and into the right loop, exiting just behind the right exit cords. Sew the left exit cords to the back of the piece at the point where they diagonally extend down toward the right bottom loop. Sew the right exit cords at the back of the piece ½ inch or so below where the left exit cords cross over it. Now that you've sewn all of the exit points behind the top of the piece, check out the top corners to see if they need any extra sewing reinforcement. Again, lift the piece to check if there are any other places to secure.

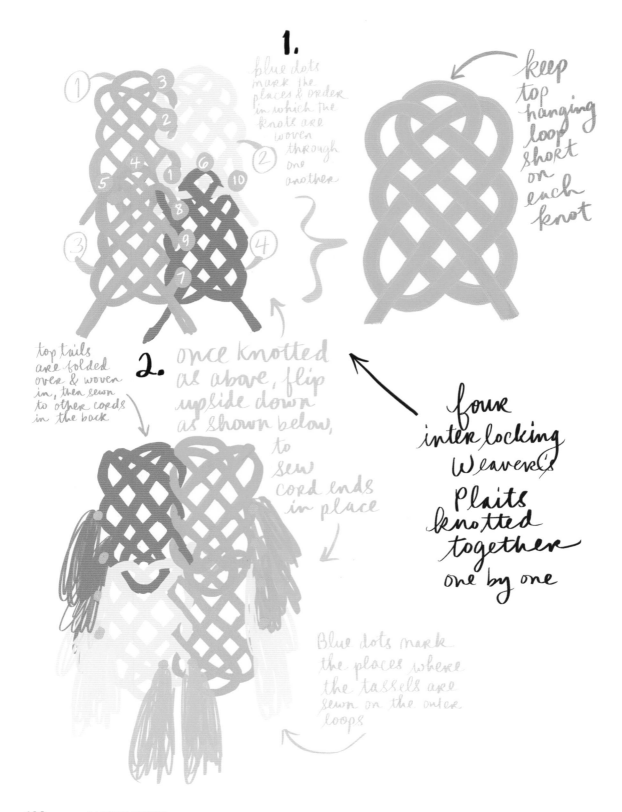

1.

blue dots mark the places & order in which the knots are woven through one another

keep top hanging loop short on each knot

2. once knotted as above, flip upside down as shown below, to sew cord ends in place

top tails are folded over & woven in, then sewn to other cords in the back

four interlocking Weaver's Plaits knotted together one by one

Blue dots mark the places where the tassels are sewn on the outer loops

9　Once the piece is sewn, hang it on a wall from two nails or pushpins under the top corner pieces and do a final check. Look for any areas that are sewn too tight or knotted too loose. At this point, you can always cut the thread and reposition the rope. When everything looks good, clip the long cord ends. Clip each of the top cord ends 1 to 2 inches below the anchor points. For the cords exiting at the center of the piece, clip the ends 3 inches or so from their exit points so they are long enough to remain tucked behind the piece. You can sew these center exit cords to the back of the piece if you wish, but they should actually remain lying flat behind the piece without a problem if they are not sewn.

10　Make the tassels following the instructions on page 67, wrapping each around the cardboard 20 to 130 times until you think you have a substantial tassel. Make two tassels in each color, wrapped an equal number of times around the cardboard. If you are using fibers of different weights, you may need to use a different number of wraps to achieve the same thickness. (I wrapped the Quince & Co. yarn 48 times; the Knit Collage yarn, 32 times; the Mirasol Ushya yarn, 22 times; and the Amano Puna yarn, 130 times.) Using the color that corresponds to the matching cord, sew the tassels at the points noted on the diagram; the Quince & Co. light pink yarn cascades from the two points at the bottom of the piece.

11　To hang the completed wall hanging, place a tack or nail under each of the top outer loops. Use a wide-tooth comb to groom the tassels (see page 71).

DOUBLE COIN CURTAIN

This project is a fun twist that shows the overlap between different styles of knotting. The result is a large piece measuring 57 inches tall by 48 inches wide. With a nod to macramé, you can translate any of the knots in this book to a flat textile surface. Unlike most projects in this book, you will need a bar to attach the rope to create this piece. The bar you choose could be a copper pipe, a wooden dowel from a hardware store, or a fallen and sanded branch from a tree in your neighborhood. If you haven't tried macramé before, this is a great piece to get your feet wet with the unique format. As you will see, knotting across vertically hanging ropes will feel quite different than knotting over a board or table. If you happen to be an experienced macramé crafter, this piece might serve as a refreshing twist on the more typical hitches and square knot variations that make up the majority of macramé projects.

You can develop endless variations on this project by shifting the cord choice, cord diameter, bar choice, knotting pattern, and cord color. By calculating the section widths and knot lengths, you could also make a wall hanging that's narrower, wider, shorter, or longer. You can also incorporate large tubes (such as pipe fittings found at the hardware store) by slipping them on the cord as you knot, or you may want to sew charms in the centers of the knots. You can dye the rope prior to beginning the project, or dip dye the entire curtain when you are done for an ombré effect.

One 200-foot spool ½-inch cotton braid cord

One 48-inch-long wooden dowel, copper pipe, or other rod

One 10 x 4-inch piece cardboard

Thread in a color that matches your rope

Sharp needle

Comb for grooming tassels

Suggested: Spray bottle with water

Variety of yarn for tassels

(I used the following:

2 skeins AVFKW Even Tinier Annapurna in Petroglyph

1 skein Cormo Fingering Purity in Bare by Sincere Sheep

1 cone Sugar 'n Cream in Ecru

1 skein Bernat Handicrafter in Off White

1 skein Anzula Meridian in Rosebud

1 skein Blue Sky Fibers Baby Alpaca Yarn in Petal Pink)

Optional: One 60 x 60-inch garment rack on wheels

lark's head

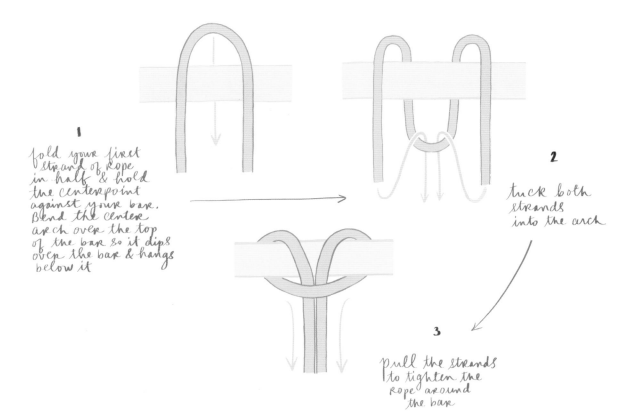

1 fold your first strand of rope in half & hold the centerpoint against your bar. Bend the center arch over the top of the bar so it dips over the bar & hangs below it

2 tuck both strands into the arch

3 pull the strands to tighten the rope around the bar

You can create a Reverse Lark's Head by flipping the bar to work from the back instead of the front.

OR

follow these diagrams imagining that you are standing on the other side of the bar, holding the folded rope pressed against the back of the bar (instead of the front). Bend the arch toward you, folded over the top of the bar.

1   To set up your workspace, I recommend you use rope or string to tie the dowel to the rack on each side, leaving a gap of a few inches between the rack rod and the dowel. Working on a garment rack allows you to move in all directions around the piece and to pull on the rope as necessary. While you can affix the bar to a wall to work, the pull involved in knotting with such heavy rope can cause it to fall or pull out the hardware. It can also be frustrating if the wall is hitting the back of your hand as you are knotting. Your orientation toward the piece can vary according to your comfort. For the top row of knotting you may want to be standing or sitting on a high stool. As you work down the curtain you can transition to sitting on a cushion on the floor.

2   Prepare the rope by measuring and cutting it into seven 300-inch-long strands. The easiest form of measurement is to pull the rope upward from the spool while running a long tape measure (tailor's tape measure) along the piece until you reach 300 inches. Once you cut that first piece, use it as a length template instead of the tape measure. Fold each of the seven strands of rope in half and, grabbing from the fold, hold it behind the dowel and insert the tail of the strand through the center fold so that it creates a loop that attaches to the dowel (see the diagram for a closer look). This is called a Lark's Head Knot in macramé. If you face the dowel from the back, and begin tying the knot from that side, it becomes the Reverse Lark's Head Knot. Either direction for the Lark's Head is fine to make the front of your curtain; mine is created with the Reverse Lark's Head Knot facing forward. Space each Lark's Head Knot 3¼ inches apart so the sections of rope are neatly spaced and hanging straight down in vertical rows.

3   To begin the first row of knots, start on the far right or far left side of the knot curtain and measure 4 inches down from the bottom of the hitch; your first knot row will line up here. Working left to right, or right to

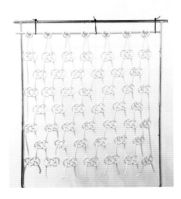

left, weave a Double Coin Knot using the two cords in each section (see the diagram on page 45). Repeat this knot for each section of rope; you will end with a row of seven Double Coin Knots. Keep the knot size and spacing consistent by making sure each knot is approximately 5 inches wide and 3 inches apart. I don't measure much as I go. I like to carry on the momentum and estimate the distance then tighten and adjust after I finish the piece. With most large macramé projects, adjustments after the fact are tough so it's best to nail the exact proportions as you knot; however, this project is very forgiving, and you can perfect the spacing at the end and even remove and redo a section if need be.

4   Start at the left or right end of your wall hanging to begin Row 2. Skip the outermost strand of hanging rope and make a Double Coin Knot using the second and third strands. This resulting knot joins two sections at their innermost strands. Working across the second row, you will end up with six Double Coin Knots, each joining neighboring sections together on the innermost strands. Now, you will begin to see this alternating pattern take shape. Continue in this pattern until you have created seven rows.

5   The final piece is quite beautiful with no other adornment—a bewildering landscape of knots. Of course, you could leave your piece in this minimalist form by just cutting the bottom tails 4 inches or so below the last row of knots, but for this version, let's add the tassels.

6   Using a cardboard piece, create tassels measuring 10 inches long. If you are using different kinds of fibers with different weights, you will need a different number of wraps to achieve the same thickness in each of the tassels. I made forty-six tassels as follows:

8 tassels in AVFKW, wrapping each 110 times

8 tassels in Bernat Handicrafter, wrapping each 80 times

8 tassels in Cormo Fingering, wrapping each 110 times

5 tassels in Anzula Meridian, wrapping each 150 times

14 tassels in Sugar 'n Cream, wrapping each 80 times

3 tassels in Blue Sky Fibers, wrapping each 90 times

7 Once you cut the tassel bundle off the cardboard, tie up the bundle as usual and pin it to its corresponding position at the bottom exit points of each knot. Follow the colors as photographed or feel free to mix up the colors in any way you choose. Sew each tassel to the knot using a needle and thread. When the tassels are sewn, use a spray bottle and comb (or just a dampened comb) to lightly brush the tassel strands into place. Cut each one in the shag style, allowing the tassels to take a wild, organic shape that softens the calculated repetition of the knots. If you prefer a very clean, geometric look, give each tassel a blunt cut: choose a length and measure the spot on each tassel to keep the length consistent, then move across your piece cutting the tassels into shape. I suggest taking several steps back every so often to check the proportions and consistency of your work.

8 To finish, tape off the rope ends about 4½ inches below the tassel. Cut the yarn, then remove the remaining tape. Remove the bar from the garment rack and hang it on the wall, either resting it on four extra-long, thick nails or curtain rod brackets. Alternately, tie heavy string, such as jute or fishing line, to each side of the dowel and suspend the center of the string from a heavy-duty nail.

KNOT APPLIQUÉ JACKET

Knotted embellishments have been added to clothing perhaps since the beginning of garments themselves. Robes and cloth, one of the earliest forms of body coverings, often had knotted belts, straps, or harnesses to hold them to the body. Later, North African macramé knotting was added to the edges of shawls and dresses; Japanese and British military costumes were embellished with knots to convey ranking and distinction; and Chinese tailors created button knots and ornate frog closures to fasten coats, blouses, and dresses. The incorporation of knots into historical fashion shows us the vast possibilities of applications. Knotting can become textiles (macramé), clothing fasteners (buttons, belts, and clasps), design elements (draping and gathering), and status insignia (military ranking). Knotted elements can be removable accessories or intrinsic to the construction of the item.

Inspired by these traditions, I wanted to consider a modern application for the back of a jacket where a patch might be placed. Any mat knot can be used in place of the one seen here. This particular design alters our perception of the knot in a way that even seasoned beginners who have mastered the knot would not be able to identify it. I simply turned a Double Coin Knot on its side so it would take on a very different look. It is exciting to consider how much mileage you can get out of just a few knots by using your imagination to shift their direction or proportion.

You can create endless customizable variations to this jacket idea through the panel sizes, colors, cord materials, and knot designs. You may also want to make your own do-it-yourself tube yarn in a fabric texture and color of your choice. In that case I would recommend making a tube ½ inch to 1½ inches in diameter in scrap fabric to prototype it first to find the length you need. Remember, as you add more strands, the strand lengths vary dramatically because strands forming the inside of the knot will follow a shorter pathway than the strands on the outside of the knot.

Jacket in a thick fabric like denim or corduroy

1 skein chunky tube yarn, 1–1½ inches in diameter, manufactured or handmade

½ yard felt fabric (or a piece that fits the size of the back panel of the jacket)

Between/quilting needle

Thread in a color matching your felt fabric

Optional: Fabric spray adhesive

Optional: Sewing machine

Plan to create this project at a large table where you can spread the jacket in front of you and plug in your sewing machine if you are using one. If you are making your own tube yarn, start here. If you are using tube yarn you have purchased, skip to the next section to begin knotting.

Homemade Tube Yarn

1   Determine the diameter of the tubes and how many strands you want to layer for the knot based on the size of your jacket back panel. I suggest creating three tubes that are 1½ inches in diameter in the width of your fabric yard, which is generally 44 to 60 inches long. For most jacket panel sizes, 44-inch tubes will suffice. Shorter fabric strips can be sewn together to make a long continuous tube prior to stuffing.

2   Cut 4-inch-wide strips across the longest side of the fabric to make the tubes. Fold the fabric strips lengthwise like sleeves with right sides together and pin the edges to create a ¼-inch seam allowance. Cut as many strips as you need to ensure your knot will fill up your jacket panel. Using a sewing machine, sew a zigzag stitch along the pinned edge to create the fabric tube, carefully removing the pins before they arrive at your needle. Once the tubes are sewn, use a crochet hook to flip the tube inside out, so the right side of the fabric is now showing.

Stuffing the Fabric Tubes

1   From a thin piece of cardboard (like the back of a notepad), form a cardboard tube by taping or stapling it to the perfect diameter to fit inside the fabric tube. Alternately, slice a cardboard paper towel tube down the side and tape it to size. Roll up another similar piece of cardboard into a tight spiral tube to make a makeshift dowel that nearly fills the cardboard tube.

The hollow cardboard tube is going to help you stuff the fabric tube, and the rolled-up cardboard "stick" is going to push the stuffing into the tube. Squeeze the cardboard tube at least halfway into the fabric tube. Take generous chunks of fiberfill, breaking it up with your hand first to make it less dense, and stuff it deep into the fabric tube through the cardboard tube. Push the stuffing with the cardboard stick as you go. Continue to stuff until the fiberfill snakes to the bottom and fills the tube sufficiently. Don't overfill the tubes or they will be too stiff to bend for the knots. Fill each strip equally and set them aside.

Cutting the Felt and Tying the Knot

1   To prepare the surface that will serve as the background of the knot, cut the felt to the exact size and dimension of the back panel of your jacket. You might opt to do this by placing the fabric on top of the back of your jacket and tracing a piece of chalk around the perimeter of the back panel as you feel it through the fabric. Cut out the shape you have traced and lay it on the back panel.

2   Lay out the knot on the back panel to gauge how many strands you want and how long the strands need to be (if you want to do a more complicated knot, you will need much thinner cord). The knot pictured is a Double Coin Knot turned on its side, either knotted with its hanging loop cut or knotted from two parallel separate strands to create four exit points instead of two. For my Levi's size small jacket panel, I needed 44 inches for the outermost strand, but only 38 inches for the innermost strand. If you are using the suggested 1-inch-wide tube yarn, cut two pieces measuring 44 inches long. We will start with two strands; you can weave in more strands if you need more plumpness to fill the back panel of your jacket.

3   You can create the knot in one of two ways: (1) knot a Double Coin in the folded construction method from a long piece of tubing that measures 88 inches, then cut the hanging loop when you're done; or (2) knot a Double Coin from two separate parallel A and B sides. If you are using your own homemade fabric tubes, try Option 2 so you can skip sewing tubes together to make a continuous strand only to have to cut them apart. If you are using manufactured tube yarn, cut a strand of tube measuring 88 inches (adjust to slightly more or less depending on the size of your jacket panel). Weave a Double Coin Knot following the diagram on page 45 to a width that measures just a few inches shorter than the height of your jacket panel. Both exit cords and the hanging loop should extend at least 4 inches from the knot.

4   Once the knot is complete, turn it on its side so the hanging loop is on the right and the exit cords are on the left, and lay it on top of the fabric panel to get a rough estimate of sizing. The width of the knot now becomes the height, and the hanging loop cords will be cut to form the cords that extend into the top right and bottom right corners of your jacket panel. The jacket panel in my example is 17½ inches high, so my Double Coin Knot had to extend 13 inches wide with exit cord tails and a hanging loop measuring at least 6 inches long (which I later trimmed down to fit the panel).

5   When you have found the right proportions for the knot centered in your jacket panel, cut the hanging loop in the center and mold the knot to match the panel; the exit cords should extend into each opposite corner like an X. Because the hanging loop is now cut, the knot consists of two totally separate A and B strands linking together; they are no longer connected by the hanging loop. To double or triple the strands, you'll need to weave in the A and B strands separately, starting in a

corner and following the overs and unders to the other corner on the same side of the jacket panel. Note that you can weave in strands without first cutting them from the skein by following the pathway of the strand from the tail through the exit point, pulling more tubing off the skein as you weave through the knot. Snip the yarn near the skein after you reach the end.

6   My jacket has a tapered panel (as most denim jackets do) with the top seam measuring 12½ inches and the bottom seam measuring 7¼ inches. To compensate for the taper, I weaved in a third strand on only the top half of my panel (or B side of my knot), entering through the top right panel corner, curving toward the bottom, and exiting at the top left of my jacket panel. Notice, the A side of the knot (bottom half of the panel) only has two strands. Set aside the finished knot to prepare the felt surface.

Assembly

1   If you are using fabric spray adhesive, spray the back panel of your jacket and align the felt to the panel by matching the corners. Rest the felt lightly on top, quickly smoothing out the wrinkles and bumps. Lay the knot in position on top of the felt and pin it in place. If you opt not to use fabric spray adhesive, secure the felt panel and the knot (including the exit cord ends) to the jacket by using pins every inch or two in a line that runs parallel to the perimeter of the panel. Make sure the knot and fabric fit tightly in the back panel as you pin to avoid any bags and wrinkles when the jacket is lifted up.

2   Once the fabric and knot are in place, remove the pins over the cord ends and take out some of the stuffing from inside the tube ends so the knot appears natural, then replace the pins. You may have to remove stuffing

a little deeper into the cords and taper it by hand so the plush gradually declines toward the jacket surface rather than abruptly stops at the perimeter.

3   Sew the perimeter of the back panel to the jacket by hand or machine about ⅛ inch within the border of the fabric and over the knot exit cords. If you are using a machine, sew very slowly, stopping to remove pins ahead of you so the needle does not break. After the perimeter is sewn, take a sharp pair of scissors and snip the knot cord ends as close to the perimeter seam as possible. The knot and fabric panel should be sufficiently taut, but to keep the knot flat to the jacket, sew a few invisible stitches in the center of the jacket through the knot. To do so, thread a needle with approximately 8 inches of doubled thread knotted at the ends. Insert the needle through the inside of the back of the jacket and exit out of the fabric panel on the outside. Pass the needle through the back of the knot and back through the jacket, exiting through the inside of the jacket. Create a double knot inside the jacket to end the stitch. Use this same technique to add four additional stitches between the center and the four corners of the knot.

PART THREE

KNOTTING AS A PERSONAL PRACTICE

A creative practice is first and foremost personal. If it's not tailored for your life, it's probably not something you will stick with, so identifying what you need and desire and how you can realistically accomplish it is important. Experiment with different times of day, locations, frequencies/durations, and projects to find the right fit for your practice. There's no single right way to do it—it may be working on an ongoing project with a glass of wine and guilty-pleasure TV shows for an hour after work, tying and untying a few small knots on a string for 10 minutes just before bed each night, or knotting under a tree on an early Sunday morning while everyone is still asleep. Your practice should feel realistic and restorative, not stressful or forced. Knotting can be brought into your daily routine any way you need it—perhaps to connect to your ancestry, as an energizing mental challenge, or a relaxing meditation amid a stressful week. There are so many different lineages, styles, and applications to draw from when you design your practice. Once you've got the fundamental skills down, the real fun begins when you venture off the predictable, educational path and into the wild unknown of creativity. In this section you will find tools that help you shape your own personal knotting practice.

KNOTTING AS A MEDITATION

Knotting is a meditation, and each knot is the mantra. In macramé, you typically tie hundreds or thousands of very simple knots (such as square knots and half hitches) in a pattern, creating a very beautiful repetitive-motion meditation experience. Letting your mind relax as you create chains of square knots from muscle memory can be beautifully hypnotic. By contrast, in traditional Chinese knotting you can create a single incredibly complex knot based upon a long series of instructions that can take hours of attempts before you complete the knot correctly; this too is a form of meditation that requires your full attention as you become completely absorbed in the craft. Knotting offers these two different doors into meditation.

The meditative mind-sets we can enter through knotting range from immersive focus to deep relaxation; our individual identity fades away, we feel a deep integration, a high level of alertness and concentration, a loss of the concept of time, a feeling of well-being, and a supreme sense of relaxation. Focus on your breath and observe your thoughts as you work. Having a practice ritual like sitting in the same space, starting the session with lighting a candle or drawing an oracle card, or working near an altar of your inspirations will encourage a meditative tone.

Grounding is an important word you may have already noticed in this book. It overlaps with meditation and refers to settling into your body, shedding mental or emotional weight that is clouding perspective, and allowing yourself to feel comfortable in your skin. Grounding is about being fully present in your body, feeling relaxed and rooted in your being here on the planet. Day to day we are existing largely in our headspace, processing information, and multitasking. Re-establishing a connection to your body is important in alleviating anxiety and shifting your awareness from your headspace to your heart space. When you shift your focus to your breathing, making sure to deeply, slowly inhale and fully exhale, you lower your nexus of consciousness into your chest. Take a few deep breaths as you imagine a tiny you who is firmly seated in the center of your head, getting in an elevator and sinking down to your heart space. As you breathe slowly and deeply, take notice of how your body feels. Feel a cord of energy running through you and into the earth, flowing in both directions. You may feel alive and present or calm and energized. Starting your practice with 3 minutes of this simple breathing technique can set the tone for the rest of the session. As you knot, stay focused on continuing deep, full breaths, feeling the cord in your hands, and connecting to a legacy of those who have done the same for thousands of years.

PRACTICING INTENTION

After grounding, the best way to begin your practice is with setting intention. Intentions determine expectations; so when we don't align with our true intentions, we are less likely to fulfill our expectations and are left feeling disappointed or inadequate. On your creative journey, you will likely encounter some confusion, challenging hurdles, failed experiments, and other difficult feelings to process. A creative practice is like a mirror, it can reflect back to you things you like or don't like about yourself. It may even feel like a magnifying glass, amplifying the difficulties you struggle with. You may become acutely aware of your lack of patience, your compulsive perfectionism, your tendency to quit when you reach a hurdle, or your resistance to your practice itself. All of the intrapersonal struggles we see in our practice are things that we already wrestle with in other areas of our lives, and our creative practice gives us an opportunity to work through them. One tool to help with this is writing down your intention as you begin your practice session, articulating it clearly in a sentence that aligns with your goals as a creator.

Sometimes producing a desired end result can take a longer (or just plain different) journey than we expected—that doesn't mean our journey was wrong, it just means our expectations weren't perfectly accurate. Setting intention around the process rather than the end goal is the best thing we can do to honor our journey and actually accomplish the ends we want. For example, if the first time someone sits down to learn knotting their intention is to make a 5-foot by 5-foot wall hanging, they likely will feel overwhelmed and decide they are "bad at knotting" or "knotting is too hard." It's not that they can't accomplish a grand wall hanging, it's that the journey to achieving that vision may take days, weeks, or even months. Until gaining more experience, it's almost impossible for a beginner to predict exactly how and when they will achieve a large end result. While it's great to acknowledge the grand vision and have that as motivation, keeping your intention for your first knotting sessions on learning the fundamental knotting skills you need to make a big future project is a more affirming, productive way to structure a practice. That way, even if your goal is "to make a tassel," your intention is framed as "learning how to make tassels" instead. Whether your session actually ends in making a perfect tassel or not, as long as you spend time working on the technique, your intention was absolutely achieved. By shaping today's creative session around a healthy intention, we are actively aligning with our goals and ensuring that as long as we remain in pursuit of our goals, we are successful.

Keep your intention focused on the journey, rather than on producing an end result. Your intention for today's session may be to learn a new technique, to relax, to play, or to brainstorm new ideas. You may evaluate your intention by asking a few questions: (1) Is this an achievable intention for this creative session today? If it is too large of a scope or not possible, break down your intention to something achievable here and in this session. (2) Does this intention honor my full creative potential? If your intention is focused on replicating something or falling short of a creative challenge, try to center your intention back on you and your skill set. (3) Is my intention focused more on the process than the end result? This is a personal check-in to ensure that we are focused on the deeper aspects of our practice, honoring our creativity, and giving ourselves permission to relax into a goal rather than become stressed by it.

MAKING AFFIRMATIONS

We often have music, podcasts, television, conversation, ambient noise, and so on filling up our space while we are working with our hands. What happens when we turn all that off and work in silence? If you have a habit of crafting with sounds playing in the background, you may want to block out 20 minutes or so of crafting time in silence just to see what comes to mind as you work. Do you have any self-destructive dialogue that pops up when you try to create? Do any stressful or worrisome dialogues from the past come to mind? Are your thoughts dreamy and life-affirming or negative and self-defeating? Do you feel a sense of unease that makes you want to check your phone frequently or feel incapable of sitting still? How you feel when you sit down and craft can change from day to day, as your mental and emotional state changes and different circumstances arise.

Affirmations are an important way to guard your mind space from destructive thoughts, transform your mood, and foster your creative practice. Sometimes saying affirmations can feel silly, but the negative thoughts that run through our minds are just as silly, if not more so, and downright destructive to our well-being. If you ask people what negative thoughts come to mind while they craft, the list usually includes "I'm terrible," "I'll never get this," or "I'll never be as good as _____." Crafting becomes stressful, a reminder of our supposed inadequacy, and we give up. Unchecked, these thoughts loop repetitively like a broken record and taint our practice. We can cancel them out with life-affirming thoughts. Repeat these phrases in your mind several times during your practice: "I contain infinite wisdom waiting to be uncovered," "I am a bottomless well of creativity," or "I already have all I need within." Introduce any affirming, healing statements that support and inspire. You can develop a creative practice that feels like a refuge, an enriching challenge, or even just a safe space to decompress and work through ideas and emotions. The kind of practice you create is entirely up to you.

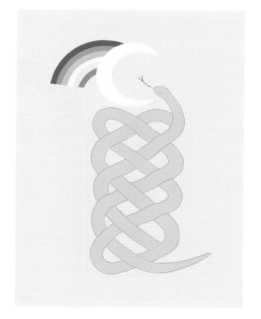

FIBER PRACTICE JOURNAL: INTENTION LOG

As touched on earlier (see page 20), a fiber journal is a place to record your discoveries, process notes, material specs, ideas, and inspiration. You may want to include doodles, observations for improvement, and inspirational swatches or photos. It can also serve as a log of your intentions and affirmations as you sit down to create. With repetitive handiwork, the mind can wander in any direction—toward worries, problems, or dreams. Documenting all of the above can be a great tool for accountability and a measure of growth in your practice. Feel free to include sketches, bullet points of accomplishments, times and dates, and anything that strikes you as important. Begin by recording the time you begin and your intentions/affirmations. As you work, keep your journal open to make notes or tape in swatches as you go. Then, at the close of your practice, record the time you are ending your session and fill in final observations.

Here is a template you can copy into your practice journal at the start of each session:

Date: _____   Time (start/end): _____

Mood (*close your eyes and breath for about a minute to assess how you feel before writing*):

_____

My Intention:

_____

_____

_____

Affirmation for Today's Practice:

_____

_____

_____

Endnotes & After-Practice Reflection:

_____

_____

_____

Blueberry Copper
pale Blue burgundy
Lilac
Blush Mulberry
Gold

purple agate
copper cord

Vintage
poly fabric
tube w/
cotton filler

KNOTTING FOR RELAXATION

There are so many different forms of relaxation that we can draw upon, and what we need to feel rested is specific to our current lifestyle or mood. Often the cause of our exhaustion isn't due to physical fatigue but rather mental and emotional fatigue. The stress we carry from our responsibilities, careers, and relationships on top of the sensational daily news cycle, overstimulating social media feed, and constant advertising can wear us down. Moving our bodies in a gentle stretch can get endorphins flowing and quiet the mind. This particular relaxation exercise is geared for those who are able to comfortably perform joint-opening movements on the floor. It is not mentally demanding, but rather relaxingly repetitive. Choosing the setting of a quiet room with silence or light music or a spot outdoors in a park or backyard might also add to the restfulness.

Exercise: Sun Cycle Movement Practice

Recommended cord: Love Fest Fibers Tough Love, tube yarn, or similar ½-inch-diameter piping cord

1   Set the tone by starting your practice after a short 3- to 5-minute breathing exercise and quick body stretch. The Sun Cycle Knot is engaging yet not too challenging and is a great knot to practice repetitively to absorb the basic principles of knotting; its intricate weaving pattern has a calming effect. Since we want this to be a nice physical arm stretch but not too demanding, I have recommended using a cord that is big yet lightweight. The gentle repetition of the design allows for a soothing task for your hands and mind.

2   Start by measuring out 22 feet of cord. Weave a large Sun Cycle Knot following the diagram on page 49. Make a knot approximately 24 inches across with big open loops. Next, take the cord end of your wool ball and pull to release slack. Begin weaving the cord into the knot you just made, starting on either the left or right side and following the complete pathway of the cord that is already in place. As you weave, release more slack from your wool ball and stay focused on following the

over-under pattern as your cord flows over and under the cord intersections. When you have completed the pathway, snip your cord end even with your first knot cord ends. You can continue to repeat weaving in strands of cord until there is no remaining negative space. Felted wool is gorgeous, and the result of this exercise can double as a wall hanging if significantly sewn to help the cords retain their shape.

Exercise: Dream Weaver Sleep Ritual

When I first learned knotting, my bedtime knotting ritual was an amazing way of training my brain, learning knots, manifesting dreams, easing "monkey mind," and tiring myself out a bit before bed. Scrolling through our phones before bed is one of the least restful things we can do due to the strain the screen places on our eyes, the reactive content we find on our devices, and the light that emanates from it and stimulates the "wake up" mode of the brain. If you would like to replace a late-night device habit with something healthier and more restful, this bedtime knotting ritual is perfect for you. Knotting became my remedy for insomnia, and I can't recommend it enough as a bedtime practice.

Recommended cord: A bundle of satin rattail

A small knot board and pins

1 An hour or 30 minutes before bed, crawl under your sheets and lean your knotting board against your bent knees or on a pillow covering your lap. With a generous bit of cord and pins on your nightstand, begin to work through the more challenging knots in this book, such as the Weaver's Plait (page 54), the Plafond Knot (page 56), or the Mystic Knot, which is diagrammed on the following page. Also called the Pan Chang knot, it represents unity and mystery of the universe. It is a difficult knot that will take a few attempts to master but is so rewarding to accomplish. The Mystic Knot is such a challenging knot that correctly completing it

mystic knot

1

lay out a "w" shape with A

about 6-10x larger than your final knot.

WORK BIG

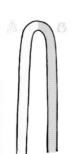

2

make a perpendicular "w" across the first with the outer strands over & the inner strands under

3

closely follow the "over"s and "under"s as you weave B through in a "u" shape

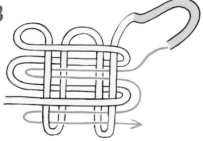

4

maintain the proportions & carefully weave B through in another direction

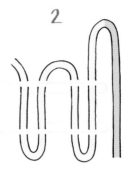

Gently tighten & shape the center,

working outward, drawing the slack out, extending the outer loops like a flower

Rotate the knot in your hand if helpful while tightening

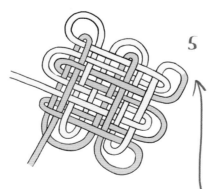

loop back & forth between your knot & the diagram to ensure you're keeping the proportions intact as you tighten.

5

(keep the cords stacked in the correct order)

as you finish tightening, Rotate the knot with tails on the bottom, the hanging loop on top, shaping it like the diagram at the top of the page

hanging loop

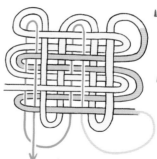

once doesn't guarantee you've mastered it, so untie it and experience a challenge on your second and third attempts.

2 Bedtime knotting quiets "monkey mind" as the hypnotic loops you create lull you to sleep. Some other magic is working too: The rope mechanics and knot meanings sink into your subconscious, so when you turn out the light, your mind will continue to knot in your sleep. Scientifically, your mind will continue any skillful activity you do just before falling asleep in your dreams, building connections in your brain just as if you were practicing it during wakefulness.

3 Follow the diagram, heavily relying on your pins to secure the cord to the board as you work. Be very careful to check your overs and unders after each step, because missing just one over or under will prevent the knot from coming together in the end. Work big and be generous with pinning your loops down. Once your steps are completed, the tightening step is crucial for it all to come together correctly. Tighten slowly and gently, little by little, being very careful to maintain the knot proportions and not yank any section out too fast or too far. A correctly woven Pan Chang can still dissolve into a chaotic tangle if it's not tightened correctly— that's how delicate the tightening process is for this knot. If you get stuck practice after practice, try to follow a video tutorial of this knot.

PRACTICING CREATIVITY

To tap into the deepest level of creativity, we are going to throw all rules to the side and embrace risk. When you knot to enter a creative zone, I urge you not to worry about the end result and instead be in a process-oriented mind-set. For this exercise "good" and "bad" are only judged by how much you can learn, not by what they look like. Leave your critic behind and enter a curious, playful mind-set. Expect that what you make may look silly, weird, or homely, but the potential ideas that arise are priceless.

Creative knotting exercises flex your crafting muscles by pushing you to understand the dynamics of knotting on a deeper level. What is it that makes cord become a knot? Is there beauty in a tangle? What draws you to knotting? The universal principles that characterize knots are balanced tension, space, shape, and form. For this exercise you are going to design your own knot. It sounds daunting, but think of how many times you have accidentally, unknowingly created an intricate tangle in a necklace chain. Knots happen quite naturally, and your task here is to get out of the way and listen to the cord.

Exercise: Design a Knot

Recommended cord: Any inspiring or interesting cord you can find!

Start by making any sort of loop you want with your cord. You can start at any part of your cord, but what might be best as a beginner is to start in the middle because knots are generally made by working both cord ends. You can go back and forth, working the right cord end into a loop then doing a complementary movement with the other side. Your knot can be asymmetrical; you just want the tension to feel balanced so that when you pick it up, it stays in place. If, when you lift it up, it starts to collapse, you have either too much negative space or the cords are not sufficiently woven to anchor it in place. If you feel more comfortable, you may want to make a loose overhand knot as if you are tying a shoe and build loops off of that. Continue to make loops off the loops and weave the ends through the existing negative space going over and under. Keep in mind that each part of the cord should feel locked down by other parts of the cord, so if a section of cord is too floppy or too loose, you should probably ease it out and reweave it or use the opposite cord end to weave over the top and lock it down.

Exercise: Design a Knot

Recommended cord: 32-ply 3 mm cotton braid cord or 550 paracord

Graphing paper and a pen/pencil

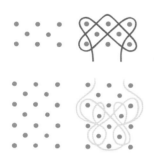

Inspired by ancestral diagramming methods like the sona, see what happens when you start your knot from a drawing. Take a sheet of graphing paper and stagger rows of dots or make dots at the line intersections every four squares, creating a grid of dots that is 20 squares wide and 20 squares tall (six columns of dots and six rows of dots). When your dot grid is complete, start to snake around the dots with your pencil, creating a pleasing line that loops around the dots and crosses itself in a beautiful tangled shape. The more instinctual you can make your linework the better. Don't be too concerned with preplanning your linework or how it will translate to cord; just let your pencil flow in a continuous line without stopping. This is your knot design! When you are done, notice that you have created a single line tangle that, when it crosses itself, doesn't depict which line is crossing over and which is passing under. Your job is just to translate this design into cord. In doing so, you will have to decide how the cords overlap each other, and you may deeply alter the shape to your liking or to create a better knot. As with the last exercise, pick your knot up every so often to make sure the tension is even throughout and your overs and unders are in the right spots. Don't feel you have to make your knot look exactly like your design. Artists have long introduced randomness into their creative process, and this exercise is just that. Your drawing was just a jumping-off point for your creativity. When you begin to translate it to cord, you have reached the second phase of creativity where you problem-solve, edit, and redesign to create a working knot.

RECORDING YOUR
PERSONAL JOURNEY

You can incorporate knots into daily life for personal growth, accountability to goals, and recording life events. Inspired by the global cultures that used knotted fibers for record keeping, I wanted to honor the ancestral, preliterate method of record keeping in a very different aesthetic and construction that reflects the eclectic state of modern fiber art. Using fiber techniques to document time connects you deeper to the present, past, and future all at once. As you document events, you create a habit that is rooted in the present with your work and life while simultaneously reflecting on the past event you are recording and connecting with the ancestral wisdom that has long been obscured, ignored, or uncredited. The piece also helps you to manifest your goals for the future by suggesting the future actions you will need to create the design you want to see in your piece.

Exercise: Creating a Personal Archive with Fiber

A dowel, rod, or copper pipe

Yarn in various colors

A variety of charms, beads, and/or crystals

Scissors

For this exercise you will create a wall hanging that hangs on a rod and incorporates knots, tassels, and charms to symbolize events you'd like to chart. As you outline the goals you want to chart, they will be represented by a symbol you choose. The desire to make your wall hanging as beautiful and dense as possible will encourage you to reach your goals for each week.

1   First, decide what kind of goals you want to chart: They may be health-related, professional, family activities, or any other life theme. Ancestral knot records recorded everything from accounting (sales and expenses for businesses) to village life events (births, deaths, and marriages). You may want to start with an area of your life you are interested in connecting to more deeply. For example, if you made your theme community, you

would probably want to track goals relating to quality time with friends and family, acts of service, volunteer work, and self-care. Outline your frequency of goals in relation to time frame, for example, two friend dates per week, one volunteer shift per week, and so on. Next, devise a key for which elements will symbolize each goal, keeping in mind the elements you would want to appear on the piece more frequently for aesthetic value. These elements could be tassels, charms, beads, braided sections, knots, or any decorative element that reminds you of an activity or feeling. If you foresee only attending a couple of family gatherings during the time frame of your archive, for example, you'll want to choose an element that would be visually appealing if it only occurs once or twice on your piece. On the flip side, if you are able to do a daily act of self-care, then you would want to choose an element that would look great as it fills up your piece, such as a bead or simple overhand knot.

2   You can determine the span of time you want to record and the unit of time the piece is segmented into. Each unit of time (day, week, or month) can be represented by an individual strand of yarn tied on the dowel (for long-range pieces) or a colorblock of yarn tied on the dowel (for shorter-range pieces). You first may have to do some math to figure out how many charms your activity would generate per time segment and how long your dowel would need to be to accommodate your time frame. All of these decisions determine the aesthetics of the piece. Of course, you could create your symbolic key based just on elements you like, randomly assign them to represent different activities, and experience the fun of seeing how your piece will look when finished.

Inspired by the exercises in *The Artist's Way* by Julia Cameron, I conceptualized my piece to archive my creative journey, and I also included some morale-boosting personal activities that are easy for me to forget, like making dates with creative friends and self-care. I had a 28-inch wooden dowel measuring ½ inch thick cut at a hardware store and used the Lark's Head Knot (see page 112) to attach 63 different sections of yarn and rope in a rainbow of colors. Each color block represents a week, and I used the following key to record my events:

Silver nugget – Artist date (Cameron's name for personal creative solo outings)

Tassel – 1 hour or more of self-care

Weaving – Finished reading an inspiring book

Double coin chain – Learned a new skill

Brass coin – Meditated every morning of the week

Brass circle – Exceeded my work goals for the week

Braid – Date with an inspiring creative friend

Brass diamond – Wrote a friend a note of encouragement

Overhand knot – Completed my journaling every day of the week

RESOURCES

Charms, Stones, Beads, and Clasps

Fusion Beads, www.fusionbeads.com

Etsy, www.etsy.com

Cotton Braided Rope (¼- and ⅜-inch)

Lise Silva, www.lisesilva.com

Cotton Macramé Cording

Niroma Studio, https://niromastudio.com

Rock Mountain Co., www.etsy.com/shop /RockMountainCo

Dyes

Dharma Trading, www.dharmatrading.com

AVFKW, www.averbforkeepingwarm.com

Felted Cord

Love Fest Fibers, https://lovefestfibers.com /collections/yarn-kits

Other Rope Varieties

Best Materials, www.bestmaterials.com

Knot & Rope Supply, www.knotandrope.com

Ravenox, www.ravenox.com /collections/cotton-rope

Yarn

AVFKW, www.averbforkeepingwarm.com

WEBS, yarn.com

Supplementary Resources

The Ashley Book of Knots by Clifford W. Ashley

Celtic Art: The Methods of Construction by George Bain

The Complete Book of Chinese Knotting: A Compendium of Techniques and Variations by Lydia Chen

Decorative Fusion Knots by J. D. Lenzen

Encyclopedia of Knots and Fancy Rope Work by John Hensel and Raoul Graumont

The Thread Spirit: The Symbolism of Knotting and The Fiber Arts by Mark Siegeltuch

TIAT YouTube channel: www.youtube.com/user /TyingItAllTogether

The Ultimate Book of Decorative Knots by Lindsey Philpott

More photos, bonus projects, instructional videos, and supplementary tutorials can be found at www.lisesilva.com/sacredknotsworkshop.

ACKNOWLEDGMENTS

I would be remiss not to thank the network of support that held me through the process of writing. Thank you to friends Kendall Antron, Jennifer Christine Williams, Mary Elizabeth Evans (whose beautiful oracle cards are pictured), and Jen Lorang for being inspiring artists, an outlet for venting, and an all-around support system. Thank you to Mom, Erica, John, Quentin, Nella, and Aunt Fininha for their well-wishes and check-ins along the way. A few artists are so inspiring that I pinch myself daily just to know them. One such is my friend and mentor, and iconic fiber artist, Janet Lipkin, who has given the world endless inspiration and me stepping-stones to elevate my work.

Endless gratitude goes to Alex Steele and Erin Conger for their very tangible contribution—their eyes and hands were essential to the completion of this project. I can't tell my story of making and teaching without including those who gave me integral opportunities for my work, like Kime Buzzelli of The End in Yucca Valley, California., Marie Muscardini of Handcraft Studio in El Cerrito, California., and Jeffrey Probart of Oak Common in Oakland, California. Deep thanks to friends who spent thankless hours modeling designs in the early days of *Sacred Knots*: Candyce Clines, Sarah Hagen, and Alexzandria.

Along the path of creating this book, I am grateful for suggestions and support from Vilasinee Bunnag, Jen Hewett, Kate Steffens, and Marlee Grace (who all have amazing books on art, craft, or the creative process that everyone should check out).

A special thank-you to Jenn Brown for her support and vision in making this book come to life.

Unfortunately, the person who I was most excited to see the book in print passed away during the process, so I'd like to also dedicate this book in memory of my grandpa Jim.

ABOUT THE AUTHOR

Lise (a Portuguese spelling pronounced exactly like "Lizzie") Silva Gomes is an artist based in Oakland, California. Her artwork and jewelry incorporate fiber techniques that span wrapping, latch hook, punch needle, sewing, tassel making, weaving, and knotting. In addition to handmade fiber work, she teaches knot workshops, illustrates, writes, and speaks on topics involving creativity, visualization, and creative ethics. As the creative community is of deep interest, Lise curates a project that celebrates the legacy of fiber called Wovenutopia and leads a creative support group called Craft & Practice. Her influences include surrealism, outsider/folk art, fiber art of the '60s and '70s, creative visualization, and mystic traditions around the world. Her work and more information can be accessed at www.lisesilva.com and @lisesilva on Instagram.